W9-CXU-784

DEFENSE
FOR
A
NEW ERA

LESSONS OF THE PERSIAN GULF WAR

DEFENSE FOR A NEW ERA

LESSONS OF THE PERSIAN GULF WAR

REP. LES ASPIN
REP. WILLIAM DICKINSON

House Armed Services Committee
U.S. Congress

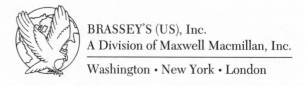

BRASSEY'S (US), Inc.
A Division of Maxwell Macmillan, Inc.

Washington • New York • London

First Edition 1992

Brassey's (US), Inc.

Editorial Offices
Brassey's (US), Inc.
8000 Westpark Drive
First Floor
McLean, Virginia 22102

Order Department
Brassey's Book Orders
c/o Macmillan Publishing Co.
100 Front Street, Box 500
Riverside, New Jersey 08075

Brassey's (US), Inc., books are available at special discounts for bulk purchases for sales promotions, premiums, fund-raising, or educational use through the Special Sales Director, Macmillan Publishing Company, 866 Third Avenue, New York, New York 10022.

Library of Congress Cataloging-in-Publication Data
Aspin, Les.
    Defense for a new era : lessons of the Persian Gulf War / Les
Aspin, William Dickinson.
        p. cm. — (An AUSA book)
    Originally published: Washington, D.C. : U.S.G.P.O., 1992.
    ISBN 0-02-881028-7 :
        1. Persian Gulf War, 1991—United States. 2. United States—Military policy. I.
Dickinson, William L. II. Title. III. Series: AUSA Institute of Land Warfare book.
DS79.724.U6A88 1992
956.704'3—dc20   92-21916
                                                                             CIP

10 9 8 7 6 5 4 3 2

Printed in the United States of America

U.S HOUSE OF REPRESENTATIVES
COMMITTEE ON ARMED SERVICES
Washington, D.C., March 30, 1992

MEMORANDUM FOR MEMBERS,
COMMITTEE ON ARMED SERVICES

This material is the product of an effort by the Ranking Republican member, Mr. Dickinson, and myself to make an assessment of the lessons of the Persian Gulf war. It is intended to serve as a precursor to a subsequent committee print that will reflect the views of other committee members.

Les Aspin
Chairman,
Committee on Armed Services

PROJECT STAFF

Rudy de Leon, *Staff Director*
Lawrence J. Cavaiola, *Deputy Staff Director*
Williston B. Cofer, *Senior Professional Staff Member*
Robert E. Schafer, *Professional Staff Member*
Archie D. Barrett, *Professional Staff Member*
Warren L. Nelson, *Professional Staff Member*
Nora Slatkin, *Professional Staff Member*
Evelyn J. Mackrella, *Assistant to the Staff Director*
Andrew K. Ellis, *Professional Staff Member*
Dial L. Dickey, *Research Assistant*
Vernon A. Guidry, Jr., *Professional Staff Member*
Lynn L. Reddy, *Professional Staff Member*
Sharon V. Storey, *Staff Assistant*
Anne E. Forster, *Staff Assistant*
Jean D. Reed, *Professional Staff Member*
Joel B. Resnick, *Professional Staff Member*
Alma B. Moore, *Professional Staff Member*
Kathleen A. Lipovac, *Staff Assistant*
Karen S. Heath, *Professional Staff Member*
Edward J. Holton, *Professional Staff Member*
Marilyn A. Elrod, *Professional Staff Member*

Peter M. Steffes, *Professional Staff Member*
Douglas H. Necessary, *Professional Staff Member*
Robert S. Rangel, *Subcommittee Professional Staff Member*
Clark A. Murdock, *Professional Staff Member*
Henry J. Schweiter, *Counsel*
Wade H. Heck, *Professional Staff Member*
Ronald J. Bartek, *Professional Staff Member*
Stephen A. Thompson, *Professional Staff Member*
John D. Chapla, *Professional Staff Member*
Michael R. Higgins, *Subcommittee Professional Staff Member*
Mary C. Cotten, *Staff Assistant*
Thomas M. Garwin, *Prof. Staff Member*
William J. Andahazy, *Prof. Staff Member*
Stephen O. Rossetti, Jr., *Prof. Staff Member*
Mary C. Redfern, *Staff Assistant*
Christopher Williams, *Subcmt. Prof. Staff Member*
Emily Deck, *Staff Assistant*
Bud Miller, *GAO Detailee*
Roy Kirk, *GAO Detailee*

PUBLISHER'S NOTE

Defense for a New Era: Lessons of the Persian Gulf War is the result of a bipartisan study led by Representatives Les Aspin and William Dickinson. Their goal was to provide the U.S. Congress with a sound basis to understand how the lessons of the Gulf war should affect future congressional decisions on U.S. defense budgeting and strategy. Brassey's (US) is pleased to publish this public document to ensure that it is broadly available to those who are vitally interested in America's role in the world.

Franklin D. Margiotta, Ph.D.
President and Publisher
Brassey's (US), Inc.

An AUSA Book

The Association of the United States Army, or AUSA, was founded in 1950 as a not-for-profit organization dedicated to education concerning the role of the U.S. Army, to providing material for military professional development, and to the promotion of proper recognition and appreciation of the profession of arms. Its constituencies include those who serve in the Army today, including Army National Guard, Army Reserve, and Army civilians, and the retirees and veterans who have served in the past, and all their families. A large number of public-minded citizens and business leaders are also an important constituency. The Association seeks to educate the public, elected and appointed officials, and leaders of the defense industry on crucial issues involving the adequacy of our national defense, particularly those issues affecting land warfare.

In 1988 AUSA established within its existing organization a new entity known as the Institute of Land Warfare. Its purpose is to extend the educational work of AUSA by sponsoring scholarly publications, to include books, monographs, and essays on key defense issues, as well as workshops and symposia. Among the volumes chosen for designation as "An AUSA Institute of Land Warfare Book" are both new texts and reprints of titles of enduring value that are no longer in print. Topics include history, policy issues, strategy, and tactics. Publication as an AUSA Book does not indicate that the Association of the United States Army and the publisher agree with everything in the book, but does suggest that the AUSA and the publisher believe this book will stimulate the thinking of AUSA members and others concerned about important issues.

CONTENTS

PREFACE

IN AUGUST 1990, Iraqi forces directed by Saddam Hussein poured over the border into Kuwait. The ensuing crisis led to war — the first major military clash of the post–Cold War era.

For 43 days in early 1991, the armed forces of the United States and a multi-national coalition fought a successful military campaign to expel Saddam Hussein's forces from Kuwait.

It is vital that we fully understand the lessons of the war in Southwest Asia and what they mean for our future. In the months after hostilities ceased, the House Armed Services Committee conducted hundreds of interviews with nearly 1,000 individuals who experienced the war firsthand.

The committee is grateful to Secretary of Defense Dick Cheney, for making the military personnel who planned and implemented Operations Desert Shield/Desert Storm available for interview. Without his assistance and that of the staff within the Office of the Secretary of Defense, our effort would not have been possible.

One of the most important lessons to be learned is that this war was unique in many ways. Many of its most salient features—not least the foolhardiness of our adversary—are not likely to be repeated in future conflicts. Nevertheless, we strongly believe that Operations Desert Shield/Desert Storm has given us, as we say in our report, "an unprecedented and invaluable opportunity to measure, challenge and adjust the policies and assumptions that will drive U.S. defense budgeting and strategy in the years ahead."

The publication of these findings—*Defense For A New Era: Lessons of the Persian Gulf War*—is part of a continuing effort by the House Armed Services Committee to understand the momentous changes taking place in the world and to contribute to the debate on how we should respond to these changes.

Les Aspin
William L. Dickinson

FINDINGS

(1) The decisive factor in the war with Iraq was the air campaign, but ground forces were necessary to eject the Iraqis from Kuwait.

- The mass and precision of the air campaign stunned the Iraqi leadership and military from the war's outset, and stopped most logistic support and ground movement in selected areas.
- Early and complete air supremacy allowed allied forces flexibility in the conduct of the air campaign and denied Iraqi commanders the intelligence they needed from aerial reconnaissance.
- Centralized control of fixed-wing aircraft in the theater contributed to effectiveness of the air campaign.
- The air campaign against ground targets was effective with greatly reduced collateral damage compared to earlier campaigns.
- U.S. Army and Marine forces skillfully executed an ambitious ground campaign while a Marine force afloat pinned down Iraqi forces with the threat of an amphibious landing in Kuwait.

(2) The effective use of high technology was a key reason for both the high level of performance of air and ground forces, and the minimization of allied casualties.

- A new precision in the delivery of weapons made them more effective than in the past and reduced collateral damage.
- Survivability of aircraft and aircrews was enhanced by stealth, defense suppression, increased use of pilotless weapons and stand-off range weapons. High availability rates for aircraft were promoted by maintainability in new systems. These factors, in turn, increased sortie rates and allowed the air campaign in particular to develop and sustain a devastating momentum.
- Greater target acquisition ranges and more effective fire enabled ground forces to engage enemy forces at distances beyond the range of enemy sensors.
- Night vision devices enabled around-the-clock operations for Army ground forces, but Marines lacked this capability.
- Land navigation through the use of the Global Positioning System enabled commanders to execute the so-called "Left Hook" through open, nearly featureless desert with unprecedented speed and precision.

(3) The war with Iraq also demonstrated technology-related problems.

- U.S. forces, particularly in the air campaign, could have been more effective had there been a greater ability to process and disseminate target and other information, especially in the assessment of damage done by allied air strikes.
- One-target, one-round precision, coupled with long ranges and inadequate ability to distinguish between friend and foe, produced one of the most distressing problems of the

war: casualties of friendly fire. U.S. forces lack effective means to distinguish between enemy targets and friendly forces in the midst of battle.

• In many instances, the readiness rates and operating tempos of primary platforms such as aircraft, tanks and fighting vehicles outpaced the ability of support structures and equipment. For instance, aerial tankers became a limiting factor in air operations.

• Communications are still plagued by incompatibilities between services, inadequacies between levels of command, as well as by technical limitations.

• The military effectiveness of our existing defense against tactical ballistic missiles has been questioned. The Patriot anti-missile system performed well in its intended role of point defense of installations such as ports and airfields. Most of the questions focus on the issue of how well the Patriot system defended population centers—a job for which it was not designed.

• U.S. forces on land and sea continue to be woefully unprepared for mine clearing and breaching operations.

(4) The Total Force Policy, requiring the integration of reserve components in a major contingency, was a success.

• The timely provision of combat support and combat service by reserve components was thoroughly tested and proved vital to victory.

• Service planning was largely preoccupied with mobilization for a war in Europe. Reorienting mobilization planning to address a crisis in Southwest Asia required a hasty, *ad hoc* effort. For example, Army National Guard combat units—trained and configured for a war in Europe—mobilized and trained for Operation Desert Storm but were never deployed.

FINDINGS

• The readiness of reserve component units reporting to mobilization stations for deployment to the Persian Gulf varied significantly.

• In-theater training for reserve components in a crisis such as that in the Persian Gulf cannot be expected to dramatically improve basic combat skills but can assist in training for specific missions.

(5) The quality and training of the All Volunteer Force proved instrumental in meeting the demands of a high-speed, high-tech conflict in the harsh environment of Southwest Asia.

• A smart, motivated force proved capable of maintaining and operating the most sophisticated military equipment in use.

• The force did not place an excessive burden of the battle on racial minorities or the economically disadvantaged.

• Realistic and demanding peacetime training of U.S. forces provided the foundation upon which victory was achieved.

(6) No firm, accurate figures now exist for the number of Iraqi troops in the Kuwaiti Theater of Operations, nor for the number killed during the war, but it may be that U.S. forces faced as few as 183,000 Iraqi troops the day the ground war began.

• U.S. commanders were understandably and correctly more interested in counting equipment that could affect the ground battle, such as tanks and artillery pieces, that they were in enumerating Iraqi troops.

• Early estimates of Iraqi troop strength were based on multiplying the number of Iraqi divisions known to be in the Kuwaiti Theater of Operations by the number of troops a textbook Iraqi division was supposed to have. This number proved to be inflated.

• Analysis of captured documents may be the only way to arrive at firmer estimates of the actual Iraqi order of battle and indirectly of Iraqi casualties.

(7) The Goldwater-Nichols Department of Defense Reorganization Act of 1986 assured that all the services were fighting the same war.

• There was a single chain of command with a clear-cut distinction between military and civilian roles with the theater commander in chief in unmistakable control over combat forces.

• Despite the progress made, problems of joint operation were still experienced; for instance, in the withholding of some combat air assets from the overall plan of the air campaign.

ISSUES FOR THE FUTURE

THE NEW BATTLEFIELD BALANCE

Technological advances have made warfare swifter and more deadly. The long-sought multiplier effect of high technology has allowed individual platforms to perform tasks that took larger numbers of platforms in the past. These platforms are approaching the effectiveness of one-target, one-round accuracy. These advances have exposed and exacerbated a support deficit, particularly in trucks, tankers and dissemination of tactical information. How this imbalance is addressed in an era of declining resources will determine whether the nation is able to realize the full return on its enormous investment in high-tech weapons systems.

MIX OF FORCES

Quickly deploying soldiers of the 82nd Airborne Division and Marines from the 1st Marine Division arrived in Saudi Arabia soon after the invasion of Kuwait to deter an attack by Saddam Hussein's forces. Some of the individuals involved in this early deployment referred to themselves as "speed bumps," meaning they would do little more than slow Saddam's armored forces if those forces chose to press the attack. The post-war challenge is deciding the proper role of light ground forces in contingency planning and operations that the United States is likely to face in the future.

COMMUNICATIONS THAT WORK

Soldiers just outside shouting range of each other were often unable to communicate by radio. Pilots aloft, not of different nations but merely of different U.S. services, were also often unable to speak to each other on safely encoded radio circuits. The challenge for the future is to ensure that U.S. forces are equipped with the means to communicate with one another.

TACTICAL MISSILE DEFENSES (TMD)

Independent of the debate over the degree of success that the Patriot missiles had in their TMD role against Iraqi Scuds, the political and military utility of mobile theater defenses was demonstrated unequivocally during Operation Desert Storm. Although some critics contend that the lessons learned from the employment of the Patriot missile in a TMD role are negligible due to the low-tech nature of 20-year-old Scud technology, it should not be forgotten that the Patriot is, itself, based on 20-year-old technology.

The global proliferation of ballistic missile technology and weapons of mass destruction has become one of the most immediate and dangerous threats to U.S. national security in the post–Cold War era. Over time, this threat will most likely evolve from today's shorter-range, inaccurate missiles in the direction of more sophisticated, longer-range and increasingly accurate systems. Therefore, the question of how the U.S. can modernize its TMD capabilities to best ensure that its forward deployed and power projection forces possess effective defenses against future tactical ballistic missile threats is paramount.

MAKEUP OF THE POST–COLD WAR NAVY

The deficiencies in mine countermeasure capability demonstrated in the Persian Gulf conflict raise broader questions about the future configuration of the U.S. Navy. For the future, the Navy must be prepared to meet the more likely threats of a new era.

1

OPERATION DESERT STORM EXAMINED
Conduct of the War in Southwest Asia

INTRODUCTION

In exploring the lessons of the Persian Gulf war, it is essential first to establish the applicable caveats and limit the usefulness of lessons learned to future contingencies. As a senior U.S. commander, not without hyperbole, said:

> Desert Storm was the perfect war with the perfect enemy. The enemy leader was universally despised and his troops offered very little resistance. We had the perfect coalition, the perfect infrastructure and the perfect battlefield. We should be careful about the lessons we draw from the war.

While this may overstate the point, it highlights the need for caution in drawing the right kinds of conclusions about this war and then applying them universally to the conduct of future conflicts.

On the other hand, it is equally important to acknowledge that certain aspects of this war are directly applicable to the type of conflicts U.S. forces might face in the future. For instance, the strategic air campaign against the Iraqi network of fixed, heavily defended targets provides a strategy that will likely apply to a variety of scenarios the U.S. military may face. Similarly, Iraq's centrally controlled military offers a potential model of the threat posed by previous Soviet clients.

A final factor to consider is that others are analyzing the stunning U.S. military success as well. Many adjustments are likely to be made in the equipment and tactics of military forces around the world in the hope that they do not meet Iraq's fate.

In sum, military operations in Operation Desert Storm provide an unprecedented and valuable opportunity to measure, challenge and adjust the policies and assumptions that will provide the framework for U.S. defense budgeting and strategy in the years ahead.

Historical Legacy

The capabilities and philosophies central to the success of Operation Desert Storm were a result of the sometimes painful twenty-year post-Vietnam evolution of the way the U.S. military equipped, trained and organized itself for combat. The lingering lessons of previous conflicts and incidents were all found somewhere in the fabric of Operation Desert Storm.

The defining experience for most of the senior civilians and officers who conceived and commanded Operation Desert Storm was the Vietnam War. Its lessons and failures all formed a powerful set of convictions about how to and how not to conduct a future war. One senior commander said:

> All of us who went through Vietnam were aghast at many of the things done in running that war. And, at the beginning of this one, one way or another we were all at that point in life where we could have easily retired. But we wanted to do the job right for the country. We were told that if we were going to fight, we were going to fight to win. So we decided that if we were going to go after him [the enemy], we were going to take his head off.

Thus, many of the Vietnam War's principal shortcomings— incremental buildup of forces, fascination with statistical measures of success, divided, service-oriented command and micromanagement from Washington—were scrupulously avoided during this war.

Another powerful set of lessons learned from Operation Desert Storm can be traced to America's humiliation during Desert One, the failed attempt to rescue the American hostages from Iran in

1979. The failure of the military at that time to have effective, deployable special operations forces capable of a successful rescue mission led to a considerable investment of resources and effort to remedy the problem. As a result, mature and flexible special forces were able to contribute to the success of Operation Desert Storm.

Desert One also displayed a fractured chain of command and highlighted the existing shortcomings of planning and executing effective interservice operations. These problems manifested themselves throughout the early 1980s and helped lead to the Goldwater-Nichols Department of Defense Reorganization Act of 1986.

The Grenada Operation in 1983 had a special relevance to Operation Desert Storm. The Deputy Commander of the Joint Task Force was then-Major General H. Norman Schwarzkopf. It is unlikely that the problems caused by the operational division of Grenada along service boundaries were lost on the future Operation Desert Storm commander. In stark contrast, Operation Desert Storm featured the first truly unified military operation under the firm control of the theater Commander in Chief (CINC), as required by the Goldwater-Nichols legislation.

The 1983–84 military experience in Beirut was also marked by a disastrous fragmentation and ambiguity of command that contributed to the deaths of more than 200 Marines. Again, this fragmentation of command stands in contrast to the clearly established, direct lines of authority used in Operation Desert Storm, where orders traveled from the White House to the Secretary of Defense through the Chairman, Joint Chiefs of Staff, to the military officer in charge of the operation, General Schwarzkopf.

Finally, the fresh memory of Operation Just Cause in Panama in 1989 validated the use of overwhelming force to achieve limited military objectives. The value of this lesson was central to the approach taken in deploying the massive 550,000-man force used to defeat Iraq.

Just as Vietnam and subsequent operations were the points of reference for the U.S. military throughout the seventies and eighties, Operation Desert Storm will now be the yardstick against which the most significant military hardware and policy questions for the future will be measured. The instinctive question will no longer be "What did the failures of Vietnam teach us about this or that?" but rather "How well did we do against Iraq with this technology or with that doctrine?"

Prelude to War: No Rotation Policy Limits Choices

As the defensive force buildup continued, each service developed plans to sustain its forward deployments. Units were identified to replace the forces first sent to Southwest Asia in case there was a long deployment.

The Pentagon does not have a standard rotation policy, so a debate on this issue began in earnest. Two issues fueled discussion—concern for soldiers' welfare in a harsh environment and the realization that a rotation policy could drive larger decisions on the deployment. Questions arose about how long troops could remain in Saudi Arabia without either fighting or leaving. If U.S. forces were to remain in the theater through the spring and summer of 1991, a rotation policy would have been necessary because of the impacts on morale and the ability to sustain readiness levels.

On the other hand, early commitment to a rotation policy could have foreclosed an early military option. Beginning to move troops in and out of the theater would create turbulence and distract warplanning.

Notwithstanding Administration statements that no decision had been made, the President's November 8 announcement to send more troops to Saudi Arabia amounted to a choice on rotation. The additional deployment severely constrained DOD's ability to implement a rotation policy over an extended period.

When Congress authorized the President to use military force in January 1991, the question of rotation became moot.

AIR POWER: THE MOST SIGNIFICANT FACTOR IN WINNING WAR

The war began with simultaneous air strikes against all elements of the Iraqi military and its support structure. Bombing then continued around the clock every day. The mass and precision of the attack induced systemic shock and paralysis from which the political and military leadership never recovered.

The early attainment of air supremacy enabled allied forces to isolate the battlefield by interdicting enemy supply lines and degrading command and control links. Air supremacy also allowed coalition forces to conduct cross-border reconnaissance and aggressive deception and harassment operations with virtual impunity.

The air campaign blinded the Iraqi military and eliminated its ability to detect movement or massing of coalition forces. This allowed ground force commanders to cloak the massive movement of over two corps of troops, equipment and supplies to setup the "Left Hook" maneuver that proved so successful. The "Left Hook" was a massive movement of ground forces westward to avoid Iraqi defenses.

Finally, the air campaign drastically wore down the ability and the will of the Iraqi Army to fight. Iraqi ground forces were so devastated and demoralized by the time the ground war started that they lacked the conviction to fight for their own soil, much less Kuwait. One senior Army division commander said, "The Iraqi soldier's lack of will to fight was due very much to the [air campaign's] preparation of the battlefield. When we got on his flanks and his rear, he surrendered. The defeat of the Iraqi Army was the result of the synergism between our air and ground forces."

Air Power as an Instrument of War

During the planning stage of Operation Desert Storm, air power advocates hoped that a concentrated strategic air campaign against Saddam's political, economic and military centers would force Iraq to withdraw from Kuwait and eliminate the threat to the region posed by the Baath regime without resorting to ground warfare. These were hoped-for results, never official objectives, and they were not achieved. The air campaign did not force Saddam to withdraw and despite its military effectiveness, did not lead to his overthrow. Consequently, valid questions remain about the limits of air power to achieve largely political goals.

However, the use of increasingly precise air power permitted the pursuit of specific military objectives—such as disabling targets rather than destroying them—while seeking to minimize damage to Iraqi society. Whether the attempt to limit the war's impact on civilians was successful remains in question, awaiting a more careful analysis.

The Air Tasking Order

In contrast to Vietnam, where as many as four independent air chains of command operated autonomously, General Schwarzkopf established a highly effective joint chain of command for air operations. This design pooled all fixed-wing aircraft in the theater under the control of the Joint Forces Air Component Commander (JFACC), General Charles Horner. Using computer capabilities not available in previous major conflicts, the JFACC could match the most appropriate weapons in the pool with the targets. The result of the daily matching process was the Air Tasking Order (ATO).

The ATO created a carefully integrated campaign, choreographing thousands of daily air sorties into Iraq and the Kuwaiti theater of operations from multiple points in the Arabian peninsula, Spain, England, Turkey and elsewhere—all without a single midair collision or accidental shoot-down of friendly aircraft.

Despite its success, the process had its detractors. The most frequent complaints faulted the JFACC staff, an Air Force dominated organization, for forcing "Air Force approaches" on the other services.

Another complaint found the ATO guilty of hindering services' ability to cope with real-time battlefield developments. The story of two brothers, one a Navy pilot and the other an Air Force pilot, provides an illustration. During the air campaign, the Persian Gulf Carrier Task Force came across intelligence that revealed several MIGs parked at an Iraqi airfield. This information was passed repeatedly to Riyadh by the Navy with an urgent request for a tasking in the ATO to attack the target. The next few ATOs arrived without the tasking. The carrier air wing commanders once again contacted Riyadh to say, "Hey guys, this is a great juicy target. Let us take it out." Again the ATO arrived without the tasking. Eventually, the Navy pilot called his brother, the Air Force pilot, at Al Kharj Air Base through the commercial satellite hook-up and told him about the target. The next day, the Navy pilot received a message from his brother that said, "Mission accomplished. Thanks for the DFC!" (Distinguished Flying Cross).

Some Marines echoed that complaint and also expressed serious concerns that the battlefield preparation was inadequate and inconsistent with the ground commanders' targeting priorities. At first, the Marines took matters into their own hands by routinely and systematically diverting sorties from their preplanned targets to "more urgent" targets or stuffed the ATO with "dummy" sorties to put extra aircraft in the air.

As time went on, the Marines began removing their aircraft from the pool of assets available to the JFACC. They withdrew approximately half of their F/A-18s so they could concentrate on preparing the battlefield in the Kuwaiti theater of operations (KTO). By the time the ground campaign began, they had taken back almost all the rest.

Despite the resistance of the Marine Corps and minor problems in the ATO execution, the central lesson of the air campaign should be clear: combining responsibility and unquestioned authority in the CINC—in this case as delegated to his Joint Forces Air Component Commander—for the planning and deployment of all theater aircraft optimizes the achievement of campaign objectives.

Tank Plinking and Other Operation Desert Storm Innovations

In the heat of the conflict, necessity prompted innovation. Unlike the ponderous peacetime acquisition and doctrine development process, the press of battle inevitably generated new tactics and unconventional uses of equipment.

One example was the development of "tank plinking" to destroy Iraqi tanks buried in the sand or concealed in berms. U.S. forces discovered that the residual heat retained by the metal tanks showed up on F-111 infrared sensors at night. This enabled F-111Fs, F-15Es and, to a lesser degree, A-6s to target and systematically destroy tanks that otherwise were difficult to detect. However, the final measure of success awaits further detailed analysis of post-war intelligence information.

Many new uses were also found for the A-10, long believed by many in the Air Force to be too slow and too old for the battlefield.

A significant portion of the A-10 fleet was slated for retirement before the war. But during Operation Desert Storm, the A-10 proved effective far beyond its assigned close air support and battlefield interdiction missions.

Although A-10s have no inherent night fighting capability, crews found they could engage targets at night using the infrared seeker on the Maverick missiles they carried. Once they made this discovery, A-10s flew against air defense sites, flew combat air patrols against Scud launchers and provided armed escort for search and rescue missions.

A senior Air Force commander said, "In a low altitude environment, nothing can compare with the A-10. It absolutely decimated first echelon forces." An Army analyst added, "We found out that the A-10 stood out as the aircraft which struck fear in the Iraqis, both psychologically and for its effectiveness."

A final example of innovation during the actual conduct of the war is the remarkable development of a new specialized munition, the GBU-28 5,000 lb. deep-penetrating bomb. Unable to destroy a well-protected bunker north of Baghdad after repeated direct hits, Air Force commanders sought new ideas. Within weeks the GBU-28 was created from a surplus Army eight-inch gun tube filled with conventional explosive and a modified laser guidance kit from the GBU-27 bomb. A few weeks later, the first two GBU-28s were dropped on targets the same day the bombs arrived in Saudi Arabia. One destroyed the bunker, which was protected by more than 30 feet of earth, concrete and hardened steel.

Interservice Fights Avoided

The sheer abundance of assets such as aircraft, airfields and tankers allowed the air campaign generally to accommodate all service points of view on the priorities of the air war. Since the three phases of the air plan—strategic, interdiction and battlefield preparation—were rolled into a single, massive campaign against all targets, differing service perspectives on the "proper" way to allocate and sequence air power to targets were more easily accommodated.

The Air Force emphasized establishing early air superiority and pursuing strategic objectives within Iraq. The Navy emphasized neutralizing threats to the fleet, primarily Iraqi enemy aircraft and anti-ship capable systems. The Army placed priority on the interdiction of Iraqi forces in the Kuwaiti theater of operations (KTO). Even the Central Command (CENTCOM) was able to impose its priority on the targeting of Republican Guard units from the outset.

There were disputes among the Army, Marines and the Air Force over how best to prepare the battlefield. Ultimately, Deputy CINC General Calvin Waller had to step in and arbitrate these targeting disputes. And as the previous discussion on the ATO revealed, the Marines ended up pursuing their emphasis on preparing the battlefield outside the JFACC process, for the most part. Despite these disagreements, the battlefield was well-prepared for the ground campaign in the end.

GROUND CAMPAIGN ULTIMATELY FORCED IRAQI MILITARY OUT OF KUWAIT

U.S. forces relied on superior training, equipment and mobility to overwhelm the enemy with maneuver and deception, achieving victory with minimal allied and civilian casualties. The swift and decisive victory of the ground campaign is a tribute to years of tough and demanding training by the Army and Marines for large-scale, complex, maneuver-oriented warfare.

Deception Works

The astute use of deception kept Iraqi commanders constantly guessing the status and intention of coalition forces. Deception was ultimately a key factor in keeping a significant number of Iraqi forward units and tactical and operational reserves out of the ground war.

For example, the presence of a credible Marine Corps amphibious force off the coast of Kuwait tied down at least six Iraqi divisions. To reinforce the perception of an imminent amphibious assault, Navy SEAL teams conducted deception operations off the coast the day before the start of the ground war. Based on captured documents, prisoner interviews and the study of defensive emplacements along the coast, it is clear that the Iraqi Army believed the Marines intended to storm the beaches near Kuwait City.

The use of the Army's VII Corps provides another example of the successful use of deception. The VII Corps initially was deployed to the center of the KTO in an area east of Wadi al-Batin to mislead the Iraqis into believing that the main attack would come from the south, not from the desert to the west. That impression was emphasized by the 1st Cavalry Division's maneuvers. First they conducted intensive cross-border operations as apparent preparations for war. Then they performed a limited holding attack east of the Wadi on the first day of the ground war, tying down four Iraqi forward divisions.

Task Force Troy, a 460-man Marine phantom division deployed south of Kuwait, used tank and artillery decoys and loudspeakers blaring tank noises across a 30-kilometer front. The unit never had more than five tanks, but by constantly moving and firing from various decoy positions, it created the illusion of a much larger armored force.

Plans to Fight in Europe Created Problems in Southwest Asia

Operation Desert Storm began shortly after the Warsaw Pact threat collapsed and highlighted certain challenges and problems the services must confront in the transition from the Cold War to the new world order. The Defense Department's focus on fighting a war in Europe created deployment, logistics and combat capability problems that could have hurt our effectiveness if the war had begun earlier or lasted longer than it did.

On the day Iraqi tanks rolled into Kuwait City, the Army's "first to fight" units were either in Europe or in the United States earmarked for Europe. Consistent with a "Europe first" strategy, the Army's modernization program provided its force stationed in Europe with frontline equipment—largely at the expense of the remaining Army units. Consequently, units charged with supporting Southwest Asia contingencies initially deployed with older, less capable equipment. This problem had to be corrected in theater by replacing early-version M1 tanks and Bradley Fighting Vehicles with newer models.

Units earmarked for Europe had planned to fight in Europe using supplies (Prepositioned Material Configured to Unit Sets or POMCUS) already positioned in Europe. These units said their first significant challenge in Operation Desert Storm was coming to terms with deploying and possibly fighting with the equipment they had on hand. Unlike the Marines and the Air Force, the Army had very limited prepositioned equipment in Southwest Asia for arriving forces.

The orientation toward fighting in Europe also caused problems in Operation Desert Storm in certain key support systems. Equipment has been procured for the last 20 years on the assumption that if it could perform against the Soviet threat in Europe, it could perform anywhere. However, Operation Desert Storm provided some examples to the contrary. For instance, the backbone of

Army field communications, the Mobile Subscriber Equipment (MSE) system, was created for the confined, defensively oriented European battlefield. Even though it was specifically designed to be mobile, it could not be reconfigured quickly enough to keep up with U.S. forces in the desert. Nor could it operate over these long distances.

Using Ground Contingency Units

Contingency units from the 82nd Airborne Division and the 1st Marine Division formed the backbone of the first defensive ground forces deployed after the invasion of Kuwait. Their fast reaction capability allowed them to be deployed to the theater within days of the Saudi government's decision to allow U.S. troops on their soil.

However, the 82nd Airborne and the 1st Marine Divisions are only lightly armed and not particularly well suited for the kind of open desert, heavy armor warfare required to counter Iraqi forces. Senior commanders admitted having serious concerns during the early days of the deployment about the ability of these light infantry units to defend credibly against an Iraqi thrust into Saudi Arabia. One Marine officer noted that they considered themselves a mere "speed bump" that only could have slowed the Iraqi armor advance, not stopped it.

As preparations for the ground war accelerated, it became clear that there was no need to use the 82nd Division's unique ability to conduct a parachute drop. So the division was split into brigades and parceled out to a variety of missions. One brigade was attached to the French 6th Division, while the other two went to assembly areas in rented civilian Saudi buses. There they joined a convoy of trucks to assume a follow-on role during the ground war as motorized infantry support for the 24th Mechanized Division.

Meanwhile, the 1st Marine Division became part of the Marine force that later crossed Iraqi barriers and minefields into Kuwait to conduct the supporting attack toward Kuwait City. The Division was adequately equipped for this role, which also placed it in a position where it could have joined Marines coming ashore from an amphibious landing. In sum, the 1st Marine Division was employed appropriately during the ground war.

The employment of the 82nd Airborne Division and the 1st Marine Division during Operation Desert Storm raises two questions, however. The first is the makeup of contingency forces. They must be rapidly deployable, but further consideration must be given to their ground mobility and how they are armed.

The second question is the match between the size of the contingency forces and their special capabilities. Although sensible uses were found for the 82nd Division, its unique ability was not required. Less than a full division may be able to provide adequate capability to conduct parachute drops in the future.

WHAT THE WAR REVEALS ABOUT OUR MILITARY

High Tech Works

Technology gave U.S. forces and their equipment the mobility, precision and battlefield awareness to bridge the historical gap between planning objectives and battlefield results. U.S. forces accomplished what they set out to do. Virtually every frontline weapon system used in the war had come under criticism at least once during its history for being overly complex, too dependent on temperamental technology or not dependable enough to perform reliably under the rigors of combat. Unlike our experience in previous military conflicts, the performance of U.S. equipment and forces in Operation Desert Storm exceeded even the most optimistic expectations.

A senior Army commander commented, "Even after the cease-fire, our weapons and equipment were still running at over 90 percent operational rates." An officer with the 1st Cavalry Division attested to the reliability of their frontline equipment by saying, "Ninety-eight percent of my brigade's equipment moved 300 kilometers during the first 24 hours of the ground war. That included 116 out of 117 of our M1A1s and 60 out of 60 of our Bradley Fighting Vehicles."

Electronics-intensive tanks, airplanes and missiles performed well in one of the most harsh and demanding environments imaginable. In particular, the turbine-powered M1 tank lived and fought in the gritty desert for extended periods of time without losing its combat capability. Frontline aircraft laden with sensitive electronics deployed and operated from austere airfields with consistent reliability.

Although much of this success is due to the remarkable job performed by thousands of maintenance crews, the fears of those who advocated trading simplicity for complexity to get greater numbers simply did not come true.

Benefits of High Tech in the Air Campaign

High technology allowed air power to achieve strategic military objectives. The precise nature of the air campaign makes it possible to pursue strategic objectives with less likelihood of inflicting massive damage and loss of life on civilian populations.

High technology improved the effectiveness of several key components of the air campaign. The first is precision. Precise weapon delivery was the trademark of the Operation Desert Storm air campaign, as demonstrated by the destruction of roughly 50 military targets in Baghdad without significantly harming the other 500,000 buildings and structures in the city. Precision delivery was evident in the campaign against support infrastructure and dug-in forces in the Kuwaiti theater of operations.

Precision plus innovation yielded tank plinking. Precision increased pilot safety by reducing sorties required to hit a target and allowed the majority of air strikes from altitudes above 12,000 feet. Precision permitted discriminate choice between disabling targets and destroying them. Precision harnessed the destructive force of strike warfare into a more disciplined instrument able to achieve maximum effects with minimal force—even to the point that precision munitions destroyed hardened targets previously thought vulnerable only to nuclear weapons.

The second key component of the air campaign enhanced by high technology is aircraft survivability. The remarkable survivability record in Operation Desert Storm allowed consistently high sortie rates, which in turn allowed the devastating momentum of the campaign to build. Aircraft survivability was also increased by the successful counter-air offensive and air superiority, but these are not the focus of this section.

High tech helped survivability in three ways. The first was Suppression of Enemy Air Defenses (SEAD) equipment. Aircraft equipped with SEAD systems were singularly effective in neutralizing Iraq's integrated air defense network. The lack of an effective Iraqi air defense network permitted our aircraft to operate at standoff distances—above intense Iraqi antiaircraft artillery and infrared surface-to-air missiles. The medium altitude sanctuary also permitted more accurate delivery of precision guided munitions.

The second way high tech increased survivability was stealth. The performance of the F-117 attack fighter illustrated the great promise of stealth systems for reducing aircraft vulnerability. The F-117 was the only aircraft used against targets in Baghdad, the most heavily defended portion of Iraq. Even though they flew over 1,200 sorties against the toughest targets, the fleet finished the war with no losses. A senior Air Force commander said, "I figured that just on the first night we would lose a couple (of F-117s) just from stray hits. We didn't lose a single one that night, and it was not scratched during the entire war."

The third high-tech contributor to greater aircraft survivability was unmanned cruise missiles. Navy sea-launched Tomahawk cruise missiles and B-52-launched cruise missiles employed against high-value, high-risk targets provided CENTCOM planners with an entirely new dimension in warfare capability. The precision of the weapon and the freedom it afforded from pilot safety concerns made cruise missiles extremely useful against heavily defended targets during daylight hours. Over 80 percent of the Tomahawks fired during Operation Desert Storm flew daylight missions.

Because Air Force planners were skeptical at first of the Tomahawk's reliability and capability, they used several missiles against each target as a safeguard. However, this practice disappeared soon after the missiles' successful strikes. From that point on, Tomahawks were used against an increasing range of targets. Ultimately, about 288 Tomahawk cruise missiles were fired by surface ships and submarines in the Persian Gulf, Red Sea and the eastern Mediterranean.

Benefits of High Tech on the Ground

High tech also enhanced the effectiveness of several key components of the ground campaign: mobility and maneuver, standoff engagement, precise navigation, and night vision capability.

High mobility and maneuver warfare were central to the success of the "Left Hook." The ability of U.S. ground forces to fight a fast, fluid 100-hour ground campaign grew out of excellent training, equipment and an evolution in doctrine.

Both the Army and Marine Corps have moved away from an attrition-oriented, firepower-based doctrine toward the technology-intensive doctrine dubbed "air-land battle." The shift began in the late 1970s to maximize NATO's technical edge as a counter to the Warsaw Pact's numerical superiority. Operation Desert Storm witnessed the transplant of the air-land battle plan from the plains of Europe to the desert of Kuwait and Iraq with stunning effect.

With the start of the ground war, entire divisions sliced across the Iraqi desert at sustained high rates of speed, some traveling 100 kilometers within the first 24 hours. Massive columns of armor and mechanized infantry eventually sealed off escape routes and pressed in on entrenched Iraqi units, systematically defeating them. Operation Desert Storm will likely serve for generations as the textbook example of what well-executed maneuver tactics can accomplish.

High tech also enhanced ground forces' standoff capability. Spotting, targeting and engaging the enemy from distances beyond the range of his sensors allowed U.S. forces to operate safely with lethal effectiveness. The thermal sensors on M1 tanks and Bradley Fighting Vehicles and the sensors on Army AH-64 and OH-58D helicopters targeted the enemy day and night as well as through the thick smoke of the battlefield and oil well fires. Army tank crews said Iraqi units looked skyward and blindly fired their anti-aircraft guns, thinking they were under air attack. In another telling example, captured Iraqi soldiers revealed that many Iraqi units had no idea they were under attack from U.S. ground units until their tanks were hit by cannon fire and missile shots.

Another benefit of high tech for ground forces is precise navigation. Knowing how to navigate in a featureless desert avoided even by Iraqis provided U.S. forces with tactical advantage. A number of systems contributed to this capability, but the Global Positioning System (GPS) was the most important because it provided precise navigational information down to the squad level in a highly portable and low-cost package.

According to many ground commanders, the critical "Left Hook" maneuver would have been impossible without GPS. As a result of GPS, artillery placements, logistical resupply and battlefield mapping were all accomplished with increased accuracy.

It is somewhat disconcerting to note that many of the GPS receivers used in Operation Desert Storm were not obtained through the normal military procurement process but rather bought off-the-shelf from companies selling them for small boat navigation and other civilian uses.

A final benefit of high tech is night vision. Years of training with specialized equipment gave the Army a night vision capability that permitted relentless attack. Around-the-clock assaults overwhelmed the Iraqis, denying them the opportunity to regroup or resupply out of harm's way. Night vision proved equally useful in fighting in the midday dusk caused by smoke from the massive oil well fires in Kuwait.

U.S. Troops Most Qualified Ever

While equipment and hardware has garnered much of the post-war praise and attention, in the final analysis it was U.S. military men and women who made the real difference. Soldier for soldier, the U.S. military is now comprised of better educated, more motivated and more capable forces than at any other time in history. The outstanding performance of the American soldier, sailor, airman and marine during Operation Desert Storm proved the wisdom of recruiting a professional military and maintaining exacting and highly realistic peacetime training standards.

This commitment to quality personnel yielded forces capable of adapting and succeeding in a harsh, demanding, unfamiliar environment. The ability to take forces "off-the-shelf" and ask them to perform in a variety of settings with minimal preparation in theater has important implications. The future military strategy may rely more heavily on rapidly deployable, U.S.-based units ready to fight on a "come-as-you-are" basis.

Some initial assessments of the war have correctly pointed out the uniqueness of having a five-month troop buildup, which provided ample opportunity for U.S. forces to adapt to the Saudi desert's harsh environment and to train in theater. Thousands of hours of intensive training did take place during this period, both in the United States before deployment for some units and in theater for others. All this training undoubtedly saved lives as tactics were continually tested, analyzed and adjusted.

However, most ground commanders credited realistic peacetime training and exercises for having established the proficiency that led to victory. Courses at specialized ranges, schools and training facilities such as the Army's National Training Center, the Marine Corps' Twenty-Nine Palms combined arms range, the Air Force's "Flag" exercises at Nellis AFB and the Navy's strike warfare university at NAS Fallon made the difference. A decade of investment, particularly for Army and Marine ground units, yielded a force able to successfully execute complex, high-speed multi-corps operations with limited rehearsal.

The fact that many major ground units arrived in the theater much later than units deployed from the United States but performed equally well in combat supports this view. For instance, the VII Army Corps, a Europe-based unit, launched the main coalition ground attack only two weeks after it completed deploying to the theater.

One senior officer from the VII Corps commented:

> The corps was trained and ready [when it arrived]. The operation was a matter of adapting the corps and its people to conditions in Saudi Arabia. The corps had a large number of soldiers experienced in desert operations as a result of individual officers and soldiers who had gone through the National Training Center [at Ft. Irwin, California] and a division which had rotated its brigades through the Center.

Another Army general said, "We had a good, solid training base when we began. The purpose of our training in Saudi Arabia was to get desert tough."

Communications Hampered by Old, Incompatible Equipment

Operation Desert Storm demonstrated that tactical communications are still plagued by incompatibilities and technical limitations. At CENTCOM corps and wing levels, a significant portion of the war was conducted over commercial telephone lines because of the volume and compatibility limitations of the military communications system. Although the arrangement worked this time, it is risky to assume a strong commercial communications system will be available in every contingency. Moreover, relying on a commercial network made theater communications vulnerable to jamming, saturation and sabotage.

Communications were worse in the field. For example, compatibility problems among the services were a constant headache in integrating the air campaign. Multiservice strike packages were difficult or impossible to assemble because various aircraft communicated in different ways over secure voice channels. Secure voice channels do not allow the enemy to listen.

This caused not only planning problems, but also operational problems. For example, when the Iraqi Air Force was fleeing to Iran, an AWACS controller wanted to signal Navy F-14s and Air Force F-15s to turn off their radars to fool the Iraqis into taking off so they could be shot down. Because the AWACS is an Air Force aircraft, it was able to communicate this information to the Air Force F-15s over secure voice but not to the Navy F-14s. The F-14s continued to operate their radars, which kept the Iraqis on the ground.

The Air Tasking Order was hand-delivered each day to Navy carriers because communications links between Riyadh and ships operating in the Gulf were too limited to handle the volume required. Initially, some Air Force units also received a hand-carried ATO, but this was a redundancy measure that eventually was discontinued.

A Marine Corps general admitted that communications were a significant problem, especially in artillery fire support, because the equipment lacked sufficient range or frequencies. An Army battalion commander said it was extremely difficult to keep the 1972 vintage radios they had operating and within communications range. In some cases, platoon leaders were unable to talk on the radio to squad leaders who were a mere 75 feet away.

However, many communications problems should be corrected when the newest tactical radio system, the Single Channel Ground and Airborne Radio System (SINCGARS), is completely fielded. SINCGARS performed well in units fortunate enough to have received it before they deployed.

Tactical Missile Defenses Succeed Politically, Raise Technical Questions

Long before the air campaign began on January 17, the United States was concerned about the threat posed by Saddam's Scuds. By the time the air campaign commenced, the United States already had deployed several Patriot batteries to Saudi Arabia to defend various high-value civilian and military targets.

In an effort to draw Israel into the war and destroy the international coalition arrayed against him, Saddam launched nightly Scud attacks against undefended Israeli population centers beginning on January 18. While some Scuds missed their intended targets, others landed in Tel Aviv and Haifa, causing substantial damage. Iraq's capacity to use Scuds to deliver chemical warheads added to the psychological impact of the Scud attacks.

On January 19, the Israeli Government accepted the U.S. offer to deploy Patriots to various positions in Israel to defend against the Scud attacks. The first Patriot batteries, manned by U.S. troops pending training of Israeli technicians, arrived from Europe and were declared operational on January 20, 1991.

Since the war ended, controversy has erupted surrounding the question of Patriot's effectiveness in intercepting and destroying Iraqi Scuds aimed at military facilities in Saudi Arabia and civilian targets in both Saudi Arabia and Israel. In fact, Patriot successfully defended critical military facilities in Saudi Arabia such as ports and airfields, and ensured that the Scuds had a minimal impact on coalition military operations. In Israel, Patriot took on the more demanding job of defending population centers—a job for which it was not designed. While its technical success in this role has been questioned, its political impact was decisive in reassuring Israeli leaders of the U.S. commitment to their security, which in turn helped keep the coalition intact by keeping Israel out of the war.

Minehunting on Land and at Sea

Across the board, U.S. forces were generally unprepared for offensive mineclearing and breaching operations. One of the most serious challenges facing coalition ground forces preparing to enter Kuwait was the layered static defenses along the entire Kuwait-Saudi border. These barriers included extensive minefields, obstacle belts, oil-filled trenches and other man-made barricades designed to stall the expected assault into Kuwait and expose coalition forces to Iraqi heavy artillery fire.

However, as preparations for offensive operations began, U.S. forces found themselves woefully unprepared to carry out the specialized breaching and clearing operations required to defeat this defensive tactic. Both the Army and Marines lacked the experience, training and the equipment required for the mission.

As a result, both services were forced to compress into a few months the training, design and fielding of specialized equipment necessary to defeat the Iraqi fortifications. In theater, Marine and Army units began intensive training against dummy fortifications. In the United States, both Army and Marine acquisition systems quickly started designing, fabricating and deploying new mine plows, mine rollers, mine rakes and other equipment. The Armored Combat Engineer (ACE) vehicle was used in combat for the first time, as well as the rocket-propelled line charge (MICLIC) used to detonate mines explosively. Mine plows and rollers were also developed in the field and purchased from U.S. allies such as Israel.

One Marine officer said, "We trained seven days a week. We built a sophisticated system of barriers and simulated mine fields. But we did not have sufficient breaching equipment until our equipment was supplemented by the Israelis, who gave us pretty good stuff." Another Marine officer added, "Our engineers did not receive most of the newer equipment until the middle of January and had to make do with the older D-7 dozers and locally fabricated equipment. Most of the newer equipment like the ACE and mine rake arrived too late for proper training. Some companies did not receive mineclearing equipment until the night of the attack."

Nonetheless, 1st and 2nd Marine Division breaching operations led the ground attack, blasting open holes in the Iraqi defensive barriers for coalition forces to pour into Kuwait. The success of these difficult operations can be attributed to the excellent training regimen developed in theater, the accelerated fielding of specialized equipment, the massive preparatory fire used to saturate the defensive barriers, the tepid resistance by Iraqi units manning defensive emplacements, and finally, to the use of intelligence to find and exploit gaps in and between Iraqi minefields.

At sea, through the fall of 1990, the United States deployed six MH-53 air mine countermeasures helicopters, three 1950s vintage ocean minesweeping ships (MSO), one modern mine countermeasure ship (MCM), and explosive ordnance detachments (EOD) to the region in anticipation of the need for minesweeping, particularly in the waters of the Persian Gulf itself. In mid-January 1991, before the commencement of hostilities, the USS *Tripoli*, a marine amphibious ship, was designated to support airborne mine countermeasure operations. Although ten allied countries ultimately provided 32 mine countermeasure vessels, except for the British units, these allied vessels did not arrive in theater or did not participate in mine clearance work until after the war had ended.

The Navy and Marine minesweeping/mine countermeasure efforts also ran into difficulties, largely attributable to inadequate training prior to the deployment. For instance, although doctrine calls for the coordinated operation of all mine sweeping/countermeasure forces (i.e., ship and airborne minesweepers and explosive ordnance disposal), pre-war training was generally conducted only by the individual forces. Fortunately, the three-month period between the time U.S. minesweeping forces arrived in the Gulf and the beginning of the war allowed for the conduct of critical training and repair work.

The intelligence about the Iraqi mine threat was incorrect. Although there were indications of Iraqi minelaying activities as early as October 1990, CENTCOM decided to avoid any actions, including collecting intelligence, that could provoke hostilities before coalition forces were fully prepared. As a result, there was little hard intelligence on the details of the Iraqi mine threat by the time the war started.

Nonetheless, estimates of Iraqi minelaying activities were made and often were wrong.

Documents obtained after the war indicated that the Iraqis had laid 1,157 mines in a crescent across the northwest Gulf. However, U.S. intelligence estimates failed to indicate that the waters in the center of this crescent had been heavily mined. U.S. data predicted minefields only in the waters off Kuwait and in the deep water approaches to Iraq. The USS Princeton and the USS Tripoli were both damaged by Iraqi mines in February 1991 while operating in areas not estimated to be mined.

Of great concern to those planning possible amphibious operations off the eastern coast of occupied Kuwait was the threat of heavily mined shallow waters—waters less than 30 feet deep that do not lend themselves to ship or airborne minesweeping/countermeasures. If an amphibious operation had ultimately been conducted, shallow water mines would had to have been identified and disabled by explosive ordnance disposal and Navy special forces. Such an undertaking would have been time-consuming and extremely risky to the individuals involved.

Assessments of the capability and reliability of U.S. minesweeping/countermeasure equipment are mixed. The six

MH-53 helicopters were new when deployed and by all accounts were effective and reliable. Likewise, the reliability of the minesweeping and mine countermeasure ships was also satisfactory. Nonetheless, the Navy believes that the acoustic and magnetic signatures of the ocean minesweeping ships are inferior to those of our allies. Moreover, there were reliability problems with the ocean minesweeping ship's SQQ-14A minehunting sonar and the remotely operated minehunting vehicle when deployed in strong currents. Finally, there was only one secure voice circuit available for numerous vessels, including the ocean minesweeping ships and the mine countermeasure ship, that too often resulted in messages being passed between ships on unsecured VHF radios.

The significant Iraqi mine threat contributed to CENTCOM's decision not to conduct an amphibious landing on the beaches of Kuwait. CENTCOM planners estimated that it would take 10-14 days to clear the necessary Iraqi mines and to prepare the Kuwaiti beaches for such a landing, which decisionmakers judged to be too long. Of perhaps even greater concern was the potential for high casualties if such an amphibious landing were undertaken under the conditions existing at sea and on the beach at the time.

Counting the Iraqi Army

After the war ended, a controversy erupted over the numbers of Iraqi military personnel in the Kuwaiti Theater of Operations (KTO) and the numbers of Iraqis killed in the war. Dependable counts did not exist, which caused unease among the American public. How could we determine how many of our own troops to send without knowing how many Iraqi soldiers there were?

There were two reasons people were not counted. First, CENTCOM did not believe soldiers were the most important measure of Iraqi military strength. The coalition command felt the numbers of tanks, armored personnel carriers and artillery pieces provided the best measure of Iraqi power. A tank unit with no tanks ceased to pose a threat regardless of how many men were on the rolls. The command's goal was to destroy equipment, so it was equipment numbers the command sought.

U.S. intelligence had the responsibility of determining the Iraqi military order of battle—the numbers and types of units, their equipment and location. Substantial resources had been devoted to that effort all through the 1980–88 Iran-Iraq war. There was less focus on the order of battle after the 1988 ceasefire, but the assignment never lapsed.

When the Iraqi Army began mobilizing against Kuwait in mid-July of 1990, interest in the Iraqi order of battle soared. This produced an accurate day-to-day reading of the numbers of units in what was to become the KTO despite severe limitations on the conventional means of gathering data—listening in on enemy communications and taking photos from reconnaissance planes overhead. It was difficult to listen in because the Iraqi Army was extremely disciplined about communications, punishing communicators who used the radio waves for classified information. In addition, the Iraqis made heavy use of buried telephone lines and motorcycle couriers.

It was also difficult because Washington, concerned with avoiding any situation that could lead prematurely to war, decided not to fly any reconnaissance aircraft over Iraq or occupied Kuwait during Operation Desert Shield.

CENTCOM's second reason for keeping the focus away from people counts was a fear of reliving the preoccupation with statistics on enemy strengths and casualties that developed during the Vietnam War. The commander of Operation Desert Storm had no intention of beginning another war defined by body counts. Still, there was a public demand for this kind of information in

Operations Desert Shield/Desert Storm. To arrive at a figure for the number of Iraqi troops in the KTO, the Pentagon public affairs office did some simple arithmetic. The number of divisions in the theater—42—was known with some certainty. This number was multiplied by the number of men thought by intelligence analysts to comprise a division.

The estimated personnel complement of an Iraqi division had been revised downward shortly before the estimate was made public. The revision had reduced the number of support troops thought to be associated with a division. When the multiplication was done, it produced an estimate of approximately 547,000 Iraqi troops in the KTO. This prompted some confusion because the earlier, higher estimate of men per division had leaked unofficially. The best estimate, however, was the figure of 547,000, which was not very good in any case. In fact, the one certainty is that there never really were 547,000 Iraqi troops in theater because—and this was not known until after the war—many units were sent to the theater substantially understrength.

While CENTCOM rightly felt troop counts were not necessary, solid post-war information is very useful. Knowing how many of the enemy were killed is politically important; knowing how many Iraqi troops were in theater when the ground attack began is militarily important for future contingencies. A credible figure would help answer more definitively questions about the role of air power in the war. We would know how air power devastated the ground forces, either by killing them or by so affecting their morale that they deserted their posts and abandoned their equipment. We would know how strong an army the coalition ground forces swept aside.

At this point, no one knows—not even Saddam. Interviews with captured Iraqi officers revealed that many of them lied about their daily strength so their superiors would not know how miserably they had failed in keeping their units intact. Captured documents offer another source of information, but little analysis had been done at the time research for this analysis was conducted. Eventually, there may be a reasonably hard figure on the number of Iraqis killed and the number of soldiers in theater when the ground campaign started. In the meantime, an attempt can be made to make a closer estimate of opposing troop strengths and casualties.

Table I lists seven relevant categories for assessing Iraqi strength. Some of the estimates emerge from hard data, others are mere guesses. But the key point is that all seven categories must be considered together. Estimates of Iraqi dead cannot be intelligently dealt with in isolation from the estimates for deserters or escapees. Because we are starting with the figure of 547,000 as the notional number of Iraqi troops assigned to the KTO, the categories must account for that figure; that is, they must add up to 547,000.

A change in any one number above must by definition change at least one other number because the total must come to 547,000.

It is possible, however, that when 700,000 allied troops attacked on the ground February 23, they faced only 183,000 Iraqis—thus outnumbering the enemy 5 - 1. That 183,000 is the sum of the 63,000 soldiers the coalition captured plus the 120,000 Iraqi troops extrapolated to have escaped from the KTO after the war.

The number of Iraqis deployed at the start of the ground war could be higher than 183,000 if Iraqi divisions were closer to full strength than this calculation gives them credit for, or if desertions were fewer. The number could easily be lower, however, if, for example, desertions were greater than the surprisingly low figure shown above as having perished in the air war.

Table I: Accounting for the Iraqi Army

Assigned strength:	547,000	Table of Organization figure for 42 divisions.
Under-strength:	185,000	An average of 34 percent based on interviews with captured officers who reported their own units understrength all the way from zero to two-thirds.
Captured:	63,000	The only accurate hard number.
Deserted:	153,000	An average derived from interviews with senior POWs, who reported 20 percent to 50 percent of their deployed strength deserting — an average of 42 percent for the units covered.
Injured:	17,000	Based on POW interviews — but the range among units went from 2 percent to 16 percent. These are air war injuries only.
Killed:	9,000	Based on the interviews with senior officer POWs. The range among units was 1 percent to 6 percent of the troops deployed, with an average of 2-1/2 percent. These numbers do not include deaths in the ground war.
On leave:	few	A reasonable assumption.

Escaped at the end of the war:	120,000	The number that falls out if all the other numbers in this list are accurate. At the end of the fighting, one intelligence estimate based on aerial reconnaissance of the fleeing troops placed the number of escapees at 100,000. But because people cannot be accurately counted from the air, that number was more guessed at than scientifically derived.

At this juncture, substantially more factual data are needed— factual data that may lie in the captured documents. But for the present, the above represent the best figures; although the range in each category is substantial, the senior officers who provided them represent one-eighth of all the Iraqi forces in the KTO—a good sample. Most important, however, whatever estimates are made in the future should take into account all seven categories listed above and not treat any one in isolation.

THE NEW BATTLEFIELD BALANCE

New Thinking About Tooth to Tail

High technology has not only irrevocably changed the results of warfare, it has changed the process. Night vision makes around-the-clock warfare possible. In Operation Desert Storm, there was virtually no let-up after the first shot was fired.

As such, these changes in warmaking placed enormous pressure on the logistics system. What might have been a sufficient support system for a slower-paced, shorter war was strained in many places during the furiously-paced Gulf war. It is clear that

Table II: Accounting for Iraqi Troops:A Rough Estimate of Enemy Strength

Assigned strength*	547,000
Amount by which units were understrength	-185,000
Deserted	-153,000
Injured in air war	- 17,000
Killed in air war	- 9,000
Estimated remainder present at start of ground war	183,000
Captured in ground war	(63,000)
Escaped/killed during ground war	(120,000)

* Number of units known to be in the Kuwaiti Theater of Operations multiplied by the number of troops thought by intelligence analysts to be assigned to those units.

the old "tooth-to-tail" relationship between support systems and combat systems needs careful review.

One strain on the logistics system was caused by a simple lack of certain resources. For example, insufficient numbers of trucks and transports often became an operational bottleneck—not the combat equipment they supported. There was a dire shortage of Heavy Equipment Transport trucks (HETs) used for moving tracked vehicles over long distances, a problem solved only after a worldwide borrowing and leasing effort was undertaken. The number of all-terrain trucks like the Heavy Expanded Mobility Tactical Truck (HEMTT) was also inadequate.

In the air, the number of aerial tankers, not bombers or fighters, constrained the number of daily strike sorties. Successful strike operations also depended on aerial tankers. Tankers were crucial to all facets of air operations, and they extended the reach of practically every tactical aircraft employed.

Another strain on the logistics system was equally basic: certain key support systems lacked the capability required for their missions. Engineering equipment for mineclearing and breaching, armored vehicle recovery, command and control vehicles, and medical evacuation assets were unable to perform as expected. In particular, the M-548 ammunition carrier vehicle was severely criticized by a number of Army units as a "turtle that weighed too much, traveled about 5 miles per hour, could not maneuver in the sand, broke down all the time and held up troop movement." One artillery officer said, "We need to get rid of it. Drive a stake through its heart. It can only carry half the required ammunition load and cannot keep up. During the war it was a pacing factor in our movements and other times we just left it behind."

Former Joint Staff Director of Operations Lieutenant General Thomas Kelly succinctly illustrated the importance of competent support during testimony before the House Armed Services Committee in April 1991. He said, "I used to work in priorities. At some point, a fuel truck became more important than the tank it supported because it is no good to have the tank if you did not have the fuel for it."

Complexity of Warfare Requires Sophisticated Support

Another change in warmaking brought about by high tech is the increasingly sophisticated nature of weapons and tactics.

Adequate support for complex warfare starts with enough trucks, transporters and tankers, but requires more than that. The character of a high-tech military campaign requires reliable intelligence systems, direct combat support and intelligence feedback.

Operation Desert Storm revealed significant problems in intelligence support. Tactical intelligence, in particular, quickly proved to be a serious flaw in the support chain. The first three days of air operations, having benefitted from months of careful planning and preparation, included full sets of target intelligence. After that, however, target imagery and current intelligence on mission performance decreased dramatically. What arrived was often late, unsatisfactory or unusable. One wing intelligence officer said, "There were actual times when we sent guys out with no imagery at all. They only got a map and coordinates to find a target at night. We did continue to get targeting materials, but the coverage was spotty and almost always dated. We put in our requests, but they got swallowed by a black hole. Of the over 1,000 missions flown by [one of the squadrons], we only got back four imagery responses, and all four were of such poor quality that we couldn't even read the date to check [their] currency."

The failure of the intelligence system to keep warfighters properly supplied with information underscores the vast increase in tailored, current intelligence required by weapons with one-target, one-bomb accuracy. By comparison, hitting single targets since World War II through Vietnam required at least hundreds of bombs and several sorties.

The need for intelligence will continue to grow as next generation weapons enter the inventory. And as the sophistication of weapons increases, deficiencies in intelligence support will proportionally constrain their effectiveness.

The capabilities of direct combat support systems were also

inconsistent with the complex nature of modern warfare. Jammers, for example, have consistently lost in the scramble for dollars and, as a result, are aging and in short supply. These limitations constrain the ability of U.S. forces to put ordnance on target.

For instance, most of the dedicated Suppression of Enemy Air Defenses (SEAD) platforms used in the war—such as the EF-111, F-4G, and EA-6B—are old. Some were in the process of being phased out of service when Iraq invaded Kuwait. It required virtually all of these aircraft to support just 25 percent of the combat inventory.

The success of the F-117 stealth fighter does not negate the need for maintaining a healthy electronic jamming and SEAD support capability in current and future inventories. F-117s did operate infrequently with dedicated electronic jammers, completely confusing and overwhelming Baghdad's dense air defense system. Furthermore, because the United States will not have an exclusively stealthy attack aircraft fleet at any point in the foreseeable future, the need for a strong jamming and defense suppression capability remains.

The provision of intelligence feedback or "bomb damage assessment" (BDA) also proved deficient during the war. One reason was the shortage of tactical reconnaissance capabilities. For example, the Air Force RF-4C reconnaissance aircraft were being eliminated from the force structure when Operation Desert Storm began, and Marine RF-4C units had already been completely disbanded.

An officer attached to an F-15E Strike Eagle wing described the result of inadequate BDA:

> We deployed a system (F-15E) that was still very immature. Good BDA was needed to let us know if the airplane was performing or not. The F-15E had never dropped many of the munitions that we used in the initial few days, so we had no real

idea what we were doing. Our guys were eager to make the necessary adjustments in tactics, but they needed some indication of
what results we were getting. But no one seemed to listen, and it
took us a long time before we figured out how to best employ the
system. I ended up getting more information and more specific
mission results from listening to radio broadcasts from the BBC
than what I got through CENTAF channels.

The greater degree of interdependence between combat and
support suggests the need for a revised method of evaluating service priorities. What has emerged as an important lesson from
Operation Desert Storm is that acquiring support systems consistent with high-tech weapons may be more important than buying
the next generation plane or tank.

Striving for a Balanced Military

Another way of considering the relationship between weapon
systems and support systems is balance. An examination of combat
support revealed an imbalance between it and our combat capabilities. It was not uncommon for weapon systems to race far ahead of
their support.

In this new era of high tech, the mosaic of systems and capabilities that form military power requires a new degree of calibration
and balance to consistently deliver maximum results. There must
be a balance between weapons and support systems. There must
also be balance among the capabilities of similar weapon systems.
If there is not, the result will be an imbalance between the
demands of modern warfare and the ability of our sophisticated
weapon systems to satisfy them.

General Kelly acknowledged the importance of this problem during his April testimony. He said, "Any force that I know of historically

that lets itself get out of balance flirts with disaster. Defining what the balance is, of course, is the art and is the hard part."

Balance in the Force Structure

Operation Desert Storm also raised questions about balance within any given force structure. One example is the current and projected mix of combat aircraft in the U.S. inventory. In executing the air war, U.S. planners faced no shortage of overall air assets. However, looking beyond the aggregate numbers reveals shortages of the most useful combat aircraft and an abundance of the least useful.

Aircraft such as F-117s, F-111Fs, F-15Es, A-6s, tankers, SEAD and reconnaissance aircraft were invaluable, yet none of these aircraft is still in production. Some even face retirement with no viable replacement on the immediate horizon.

On the other hand, the F-16 and the F/A-18 were available in large numbers but their limited range and limited night capability reduced their ability to play an interdiction role. Due to the particular nature of this air war, there was little air-to-air combat, for which the F-16 and F/A-18 are best suited.

Furthermore, the limited numbers of the Low Altitude Navigation Targeting Infrared for Night (LANTIRN) pods deprived F-16s of the means to deliver precision munitions. F-15E aircraft also needed LANTIRN for precision delivery. Priority for fielding the small quantities of pods went to the F-15Es because of their range and payload capabilities.

Balance Within Weapon Systems

Another imbalance exists between the capabilities of similar weapon systems in different services. Fielding weapon systems that lack similar capabilities because of different subsystems makes it very difficult to integrate disparate, multiservice assets into effective combat operations.

For instance, under the established rules of engagement, the F-14, the F/A-18 and the F-16 could not positively identify enemy targets beyond visual range, hampering their usefulness. Only the Air Force F-15 had the capabilities required under the rules of engagement to use air-to-air missiles beyond visual range.

A Marine pilot said, "We need to start buying airplanes more like the Air Force, with the full set of gear. Instead, we buy Cadillacs with roll-up windows, like the F/A-18 with unsatisfactory radar warning receivers, expendables [e.g., chaff and flares] and [missile and bomb] racks. I would give up 1 of the 12 aircraft in my squadron in order to fully equip the other 11."

Unlike the Army and Air Force, Marine ground and aviation units had little or no night fighting capability, which forced them to virtually cease offensive action with the onset of dusk every day.

One of the most urgent imbalances between weapon system capabilities and the requirements of high-tech warfare is inadequate means of distinguishing enemy from friendly forces. The identification measures used during ground operations such as the inverted "V" markings, reflective tape and other indicators combined with permissive fire arrangements failed to provide an adequate level of protection against friendly fire. This problem directly contributed to the coalition casualties caused by friendly fire.

The lethality and range of air-to-ground attack aircraft and antiarmor weapons has dramatically increased over time, but the ability to discriminate among targets in a crowded battlefield has not kept pace. Unless more reliable positive identification measures are developed and fielded, the friendly fire problem will grow to the point where it will seriously constrain the ability to employ the full range of capabilities found in current and future weapon systems.

With the notable exception of the friendly fire problem, most imbalances in Operation Desert Storm were addressed by applying brute force. The vast quantities of equipment, personnel and other resources available in Operation Desert Storm made this method of problem solving possible.

However, the option will not be available much longer. Declining defense budgets and a shrinking force structure will limit our ability to buy our way out of problems. What is now required is more balance in our forces and systems to prevent the problems identified here from constraining us on future battlefields.

GOLDWATER-NICHOLS PLAYED A CRUCIAL ROLE

Operation Desert Storm was the first major test of the Goldwater-Nichols Department of Defense Reorganization Act of 1986. By most accounts, it passed with flying colors.

Reflecting on the importance of this legislation for the conduct of the Persian Gulf war, Secretary of Defense Richard Cheney said:

> I am personally persuaded that [Goldwater-Nichols] was the most far-reaching piece of legislation affecting the Department since the original National Security Act of 1947. . . . Clearly, it made a major contribution to our recent military successes.

Goldwater-Nichols Fosters Jointness

In past conflicts, each military service ran its own operation, sometimes without the benefit of much centralized control. The Goldwater-Nichols Act sought to foster joint military approaches to warfare by increasing the power of the Joint Combatant

Commanders-in-Chief (CINCs), streamlining their chain of command to the President and strengthening the role of the Chairman of the Joint Chiefs of Staff.

Goldwater-Nichols gave the CINCs authorities commensurate with their long-held responsibility for the conduct of a war. Most of the added authorities, such as command, employment of forces, and hiring and firing of subordinates were exercised by General Schwarzkopf in the Persian Gulf war. It also gave the CINC significant authority over logistics and support.

Unity of Command Was Key

The most identifiable feature was the streamlined chain of command from Washington to the field commander. General Schwarzkopf, not the Joint Chiefs of Staff, controlled operations in the theater. The theater commander also was in complete control over combat forces.

Because of the single chain of command, there was little opportunity to revisit decisions endlessly, as is the usual Pentagon practice. Goldwater-Nichols did not terminate interservice disagreements—it made their resolution possible. For example, the CINC made the decision not to conduct an amphibious landing contrary to the strongly held views of some subordinate Marine commanders. This would have been a difficult decision to make stick prior to Goldwater-Nichols.

In a marked departure from the past, the CINC also exercised overall control of logistics support in his theater of operations and of deployment priorities for bringing troops and equipment into the theater. General H. T. Johnson, commander of the Transportation Command, said that his command had many requests to ship weapons and equipment throughout the buildup and during the conflict. He told his staff, "Go to the unified command. If it is a requirement, and if it is a priority, we will move it. And that's the only way we get this to move."

Goldwater-Nichols laid the foundation for holding field commanders accountable for accomplishing their missions. CINCs run wars and should be held accountable for the results.

Jointness Problems Still Remain

This overall success cannot obscure the fact that much remains to be done to continue fostering jointness. The services' attitudes about combined operations have improved. But Operation Desert Storm revealed a reluctance by some to fully integrate their forces and equipment. For example, as discussed above, the Marines were unwilling to leave all their fixed-wing aircraft at the disposal of the JFACC staff for use in the Air Tasking Order.

2

PROVIDING THE FORCES
U.S. Personnel in the Persian Gulf Crisis

THE ALL VOLUNTEER FORCE (AVF)

The Gulf war tested for the first time whether the All Volunteer Force would be effective in war. By all accounts, the AVF passed with honors.

In his testimony on June 12, 1991, General H. Norman Schwarzkopf, Commander in Chief of U.S. forces in the war, testified:

> This magnificent fighting force, both active and reserve, is an all volunteer force. A true cross section of Americans who volunteered to go in harm's way in order to serve their nation and the interests of the international community. Of special inspiration to me were our NCOs and young officers who led by their example throughout the grueling days and nights of Operation Desert Shield and by their courage throughout Operation Desert Storm. The All Volunteer Force has faced its trial by fire, Iraqi fire, and has emerged a resounding success.

Background

The performance of the AVF in the Gulf war may have surprised those who remembered the problems of the 1970s. In 1973 the United States had established an all volunteer force based on marketplace incentives—good pay and benefits for all who volunteered. By the late 1970s, the effect of lower enlistment standards for recruits and higher discipline problems raised serious concerns about force quality and effectiveness.

In response to these concerns, the services made a series of major changes. Under congressional prodding, the military raised the education and testing standards for new recruits. Congress made the military more attractive by providing better pay and new educational benefits.

By 1990, this new approach proved to be an effective way to field a force of educated, experienced and disciplined people.

- The new approach provided 100 percent of service enlistment needs with educated enlistees. About 91 percent of all new enlistees were high school graduates, and 95 percent scored in the top three of the five mental categories in the DOD's qualification test. Active-duty noncommissioned officers (NCOs) with college credits and college students in the ranks of reserve component units were common.
- The experience level and maturity of the active-duty enlisted force rose significantly over the last decade. As a higher percentage of enlistees re-enlisted, average service experience lengthened from 67 months to 78 months, average age increased from 25 years to 26.5 years, and the percent married went from about 40 percent to about 50 percent.
- The people in the AVF were remarkably self-disciplined. Indications of a lack of discipline such as absences without leave, desertions, court martials and sick rates were at their historic lows—an extraordinary turn around from the terrible problems in the 1970s.

How Would the AVF Fight?

One question that Operations Desert Shield/Desert Storm asked and answered was, "How well can this force fight a war?"

The force proved to be highly motivated. The morale indicators for the force in Southwest Asia were better than in the United States. Sick call and hospitalization rates were less than half of peacetime levels; accident rates were less than half those in a comparable U.S. experience, namely at the National Training Center. A

House Armed Service Committee delegation in November 1990 reported that the farther forward it moved and "the harsher the conditions, the better...morale."

The force proved to be adaptive. The harsh environment of Southwest Asia challenged the AVF. In testimony before the House Armed Services Committee in late January 1991, service representatives cited the operational innovations by resourceful people in the field as a major reason for achieving equipment readiness rates above peacetime standards.

Support units modified organizations and procedures to meet the challenges posed by the vast distances and rapid buildup and got the job done. The 101st Division, which deployed understrength and received some fill-in, credited the quality of the individual soldier and his educational level for their quick infusion into the air assault units.

But Is It Fair?

The war also raised anew the questions of representation of minorities and the poor in the AVF—whether, in fact, it was fair.

Black Americans of recruitment age comprise about 14 percent of the population as a whole, but 26 percent of new Army recruits and about 18 percent of new Marine Corps recruits. Overall, blacks comprise 31 percent of enlisted Army soldiers and 21 percent of enlisted Marines, compared to 12 percent of the general population aged 18 to 24. It is this disproportionate representation that gave rise to concerns of disproportionate risk for blacks.

This question was treated in a report issued separately on April 26, 1991.[1] The report examined three scenarios for armed conflict, and estimated the proportion of black service members at risk. In

---

[1] Aspin, Les. *All Volunteer: A Fair System, A Quality Force.* House Armed Services Committee. 1991. Washington, D.C.

conflicts involving chiefly air power, or air power and Navy ships, blacks were underrepresented compared to their proportion of the population as a whole. In a ground war, blacks were somewhat overrepresented.

In a war of the type fought against Iraq for the liberation of Kuwait, the report found that blacks would comprise 18 to 19 percent of the combat force. These figures are lower than the figures for black representation among enlisted service members for two reasons. First, blacks are underrepresented among Air Force and Navy pilots compared to their proportion of the total population. Second, blacks are not so disproportionately represented in the combat arms of the Army and Marine Corps as they are in the services as a whole.

Black combat deaths in the Iraq war were about 15 percent of the total.

The study also found that Hispanics and Asian Americans were underrepresented in the AVF compared to their proportion of the population overall.

Where many commentators said the All Volunteer Force was chiefly dependent on the lower economic classes, an examination by the Congressional Budget Office cited in the report found the socio-economic characteristics of the AVF to be generally reflective of the larger society.

Women in the Services

Women served in greater numbers and performed a wider variety of military occupations in Operation Desert Storm than in any other conflict. More than 35,000 servicewomen were deployed to Southwest Asia as logisticians, air traffic controllers, engineer equipment mechanics, drivers, reconnaissance aircraft pilots and in scores of other positions. Two women were taken as prisoners of war. Fifteen were killed in the conflict, five by enemy fire.

As they have in other conflicts, American women showed themselves enormously capable and professional. Although they were deployed to a country that severely restricts women's role in society, American servicewomen performed their missions with distinction.

During Operation Desert Storm, American society continued to display its willingness to accept the enhanced role for military women that had first revealed itself in Operation Just Cause. While there were some undercurrents of disapproval, discussions more often focused on women's competence and willingness to serve. As a result of the Operation Desert Storm experience, Congress last year repealed the law prohibiting women aviators from flying combat missions.

THE GUARD AND RESERVE

Background

The U.S. response to the crisis in the Gulf involved the largest mobilization of reserve components since the Korean War of 1950, and the first major mobilization since the Berlin Crisis of 1961–62.

The U.S. response also provided the first test of the Total Force Policy. In 1973, following the end of the Vietnam War, the Department of Defense implemented the Total Force Policy, integrating the active and the reserve components into a combined fighting force.

How this mobilization was carried out, how the reserve components performed and what lessons might be learned for the future are the subjects of this portion of the inquiry.

Planning for World War III

Pre-war planning for reserve component mobilization—particularly in the Army—focused on a general war with the Soviet Union, triggered by a Warsaw Pact attack on NATO. The military planning envisioned a quick political decision to transition to full U.S. mobilization.

Mobilization planning did not envision the way in which guard and reserve personnel were to be mobilized following the Iraqi invasion of Kuwait on August 2, 1990.

Mobilization—In Pieces by Improvisation

Following the invasion of Kuwait, the services began preparing for action in Southwest Asia without knowing when—or whether—they would be able to call up the guard and reserve. As a result, they relied on active-duty forces and volunteers from the reserve components in developing their early responses, while laying plans to use the reserve components whenever they became available.

On August 22, 1990, the President invoked section 673b of Title 10 of the United States Code, stating that "it is necessary to augment the active armed forces of the United States for an effective conduct of operational missions in and around the Arabian Peninsula." This permitted calling to active duty as many as 200,000 selected reservists.

However, the authority that Secretary Cheney gave to the services on August 23, 1990, was for 48,800—not 200,000—and it had a number of restrictions.

- It allocated:
  - 14,500 for the Air Force

- 3,000 for the Marine Corps
- 6,300 for the Navy
- 25,000 for the Army, specifically excluding combat troops
- Active-duty service was limited to a total of 180 days.
- Access to individual replacements—vital to filling critical skills in mobilizing units—was limited to volunteers because section 673b permits no access to the Individual Ready Reserve (IRR). The IRR remained unavailable until January 17, 1991, when Operation Desert Storm began.

These initial call-up limits reflected the caution of the President and his advisers about tapping the reserve components, particularly combat units.

The specific units called up and deployed reflected General Schwarzkopf's priorities for Southwest Asia. Those priorities were:

- More airlift and sealift to move the people and the equipment to Southwest Asia (available from Air Force guard and reserve units supporting MAC and SAC, and from Army and Navy port support units).
- More support for the combat forces; for example, truck transportation, water purification, postal, military police and medical services (available from the Army guard and reserve units providing combat service support, and from Navy medical services units).

The Shift to an Offensive Option

In September 1990, members of Congress urged a call-up of reserve component combat units to fully test the Total Force policy. To remove an impediment to the call-up of these combat units, Congress extended the duration of their call-up to a total of 360 days. This extension became law on November 5, 1990.

On November 8, 1990, the President announced a force buildup in Southwest Asia to provide an offensive option to force Iraq out of Kuwait. The buildup would have two main elements—more reserve component forces and more heavy forces drawn from active-duty units in Europe.

Secretary Cheney expanded his earlier reserve component call-up authority on November 14, and again on December 1, 1990, to a total of 188,000 people:

- 20,000 for the Air Force
- 23,000 for the Marine Corps
- 30,000 for the Navy
- 115,000 for the Army, without a prohibition on combat forces

Thus, the stage was finally set for the test of the Total Force policy.

ARMY

Total Force policy finds its largest expression in the Army, whose 750,000 guard and reserve members provide about 50 percent of its total combat power, about 60 percent of its combat support and about 70 percent of its combat service support.

The Mobilization

In response to the invasion of Kuwait, the Army ultimately activated over 145,000 guard and reserve personnel, or about 20 percent of the available force.

These personnel performed with distinction and proved critical to Army success in the war with Iraq. The mobilization was not without its difficulties, however.

These difficulties had their origins in a number of factors, including the piecemeal call-up authorization, the special demands of Southwest Asia, the need to improvise in the absence of appropriate planning, the pervasive pre-war focus on a European scenario, and readiness problems with the units themselves.

The mobilization eventually comprised 145,000 persons:

- The majority provided combat service support functions including transportation, medical, postal, water purification, civil affairs, finance and maintenance.
- Some provided combat support functions including engineers, aviation, chemical defense and decontamination and artillery (designated as support because they were intended for division- and corps-level support).
- 16,000 provided combat capabilities, specifically the National Guard roundout brigades and battalions.
- About 75,000 guard and reserve people were in Southwest Asia at the peak of the war, about 25 percent of the Army in-theater strength. About 75 percent of those deployed provided combat service support and 25 percent provided combat support.
- Less than 10 percent of the guard and reserve people were deployed to Europe to provide support functions.
- Most of the remaining guard and reservists were deployed at locations in the United States, either to provide support functions or to train for deployment to Southwest Asia.
In addition to these totals, there were about 14,000 Individual Ready Reservists that the Army was able to activate after January 17, 1991, to fill critical slots. The totals include a few thousand early volunteers that the Army had put on active duty in combat service support roles.

Evolution of the Call-Up

The Army tailored its use of reserve components to meet the military requirements in Southwest Asia. The Army view of the role of the guard and reserves changed over time. These changes reflected both the constraints on the Army's call-up authority and the changing situation in the theater and in Washington:

- In the first weeks of August, the Army began planning an 88,000-person call-up of combat and support units tailored to the crisis. To meet the immediate needs of the theater for support for the early arriving Army combat units, the Army committed a large part of its available active-duty combat service support units.
- On August 23, 1990, the Army received authorization for only 25,000 personnel in support units, rather than 88,000 personnel including combat units. The Army responded by mobilizing only those units needed quickly by General Schwarzkopf.
- The differences between the host nation support and infrastructure available in Southwest Asia, and what was assumed available in pre-war planning for a European crisis, led to unexpected differences in the types of units deployed. Thus:

  - Support units that would have been late deploying in a European war (e.g., water purification, postal) were forced to be early deploying to Southwest Asia, regardless of their readiness.
  - Units that expected to be early mobilizing, such as the guard roundout combat brigades that were part of early deploying active divisions, could not be used because of the Administration's interpretation of its limited mobilization authority and higher priority in theater.

This chain of events had two results:

- It ruptured Capstone and Roundout, two long-standing programs that were the Army's principal mechanism for integrating the active-duty personnel and reserves into cohesive wartime commands.
- It negated reserve component expectations—particularly, but not exclusively, in the combat units—that the Army's active and reserve forces would go to war together.

Capstone identifies the active-duty units with which reserve units will be associated in wartime, and establishes a formal peacetime relationship between them that includes joint planning and exercises.

Roundout does essentially the same thing, but National Guard Roundout brigades and battalions are not merely associated with their active units. They are intended to make whole or round out those active units to their full strength.

It is against the backdrop of expectations and relationships created by these two programs and their associated planning that the mobilization of Army reserve components took place.

Some reserve component units that anticipated early call-up were not called at all. One such unit was the Army National Guard artillery brigade from South Carolina that is operationally aligned with the early deploying XVIII Airborne Corps. This unit was told by its active force counterpart to expect to be in Southwest Asia by September. Preparations were begun at cost to the personal and civilian professional lives of brigade members, yet the final call never came.

The commander of the Second Army, an Army element that mobilized nearly 50,000 reservists and guardsmen, called the inability to capitalize on programs such as Capstone one of the bad news stories of the war. As reported to the committee by both active and reserve commanders, the Army paid a price for discarding Roundout and Capstone because it:

- Increased the effort required to determine the post-mobilization readiness of reserve units and increased the inefficiency of the process. For example, reserve units frequently had to repeat training or administrative measures already accomplished at home station in order to prove their readiness to people unfamiliar with their unit.
- Created numerous instances where reserve component units perceived themselves to be second-class citizens in the view of active units that had never trained or worked with the reserve unit.
- Extended by 30 to 60 days the time required for reserve units thrust into new organizations in Southwest Asia to become fully integrated with the operational and tactical procedures of the new unit.

In November 1990, the Army view of the guard and reserve role evolved again with the extension of active-duty service to a total of 360 days and the President's decision to prepare for an offensive. With the increase in call-up authority to 80,000 on November 14, 1990, and then to 115,000 on December 1, 1990, the guard and reserves were now used in four roles:

- To provide combat service support units for the additional combat forces being sent to Southwest Asia from the United States and Europe.
- To increase Army land combat capability against Iraqi forces, the most immediate need being field artillery.
- To provide suitable forces to reinforce Southwest Asia, if the situation required. This would best be done with mechanized

or armored (i.e., heavy) combat units. The Army only had available parts of two active heavy divisions in the United States. Thus, the Army called up the guard's heavy ground combat brigades and battalions, which are discussed below.
- To provide U.S. and European commands with the critical capabilities and services that had been halted or degraded by the deployment of active forces to Southwest Asia.

Although expanded mobilization ceilings would have permitted the activation of Capstone units, particularly those large reserve units that had formed the principal pre-war support structure for the Army component of Central Command, the Army primarily activated elements of those units.

As the Chief of Staff of the Third Army said, introduction of all the Capstone-aligned reserve general officer commands late in the deployment would have severely interrupted a functioning, albeit ad hoc, mixed active-reserve support command and control structure at a critical point of buildup for the offensive.

Making Units Ready and Measuring Them

Even as mobilization policy evolved and changed, units were reporting to their mobilization centers making ready for war. The central question was whether they were ready.

Readiness is measured on a scale of 1 to 4. C-1 is the top, C-4 the bottom. (Another category, C-5, covers units in the midst of reorganization or being re-equipped.)

The standard the Army set for deploying combat support and combat service support units was C-3—not an exceptionally demanding standard. It meant a unit had to have about 70 percent of authorized people (number and skills), 65 percent of authorized equipment (number and readiness), and need no more than 5 to 6 weeks of additional training.

Nonetheless, as the call-up proceeded, Forces Command, the Army command responsible for providing, training and equipping forces, found it increasingly difficult to provide support units that met this C-3 rating.

- The pool of critical and unique combat service support units and skills (e.g., surgeons and nurses, truck drivers and maintenance technicians, water treatment specialists) was becoming exhausted. By the end of the mobilization period, the Army had called up eight of the nine guard medium truck companies, eight of the nine guard evacuation hospitals, all six guard water purification units and 71 of the 119 military police units. The Army Reserve had comparable call-up rates.
- The readier units were called up first. Forces Command reported that between August and early November 1990, 15 percent of Army units reporting to mobilization stations were rated as not deployable (i.e., C-4/5). From early November 1990 to mid-January 1991, 34 percent were rated as not deployable.
- Forces Command had increasing difficulty improving the incoming combat support units to a C-3 rating. Early efforts to move people from one unit to another, due to lack of access to the IRR, greatly exacerbated the problem for later deploying units. Further, the mobilization stations were running out of equipment to make up for the equipment shortfalls of newly arriving units.

Some expedient solutions were available. Fuel handlers could become water handlers. But these solutions were limited.

By the end of the mobilization, Forces Command had nearly

exhausted its ability to put together the kind of support units needed in Southwest Asia.

What Happened?

One reason for the readiness problem at the mobilization centers was that the units being called up simply were not as ready as the Army's rating system had said they were. The report that is used to capture readiness is the Army's Unit Status Report. This report allows a unit much discretion and, it turns out, was a poor predictor of how well prepared a unit was to do its job.

One guard hospital unit arrived at the mobilization station rated C-2 and, therefore, supposedly deployable. It had more than 80 percent of its authorized personnel. The problem was that it had none of the 12 doctors required by the unit.

One brigade reported itself to be C-2 overall despite being short 179 mechanics.

Many reserve component Military Police units did not have the High Mobility Multipurpose Wheeled Vehicle (HMMWV). This bigger, more powerful successor to the jeep was required for service in Southwest Asia and had to be supplied to the units.

Other units had never been assigned their full complement of equipment during peacetime, training each year with borrowed equipment.

Each unit assessed its own rating under pressures to inflate ratings to make unit performance look better. Several of the officers interviewed for this paper said higher headquarters inflated their ratings before sending them on to Washington.

The Army has a fail-safe system, however, to prevent unready units from deploying to a combat theater. Since the Korean War, the Army had required a formal validation of reserve component unit's readiness by active-duty commanders at the mobilization station before the unit could deploy outside the United States.

This prevents the Army from sending units into combat that are not ready, but it does nothing to prevent them from arriving at the mobilization station that way.

Large Combat Units—A Special Case

In mid-November the Army mobilized three heavy combat brigades and three heavy combat battalions. Although reserve component units, these Roundout units were parts of active-duty divisions.

The Army had long planned that in a short-notice deployment it would replace each Roundout brigade with an active-duty brigade. In such a situation, the Army expected that the Roundout brigades would arrive in theater no earlier than 45 to 60 days after mobilization.

Plans for extended post-mobilization training of the Roundout units reflected the Army's belief that the synchronization and integration skills needed to use battalion- and brigade-sized units effectively could not be attained quickly after mobilization by units limited to 39 days of training per year.

The Army viewed deploying these units to Southwest Asia without the needed training as unnecessary as long as more combat capable, active-duty units were still available to meet theater requirements.

Additionally, the Army Chief of Staff established a requirement that the reserve component combat units must meet the highest standard of readiness (C-1) prior to being deployed to Southwest Asia. After mobilization the Roundout brigades were assessed as less ready than the units had originally assessed themselves. A large number of active-duty personnel were committed to training the Roundout brigades.

The commanders of the Roundout brigades recognized the need for some post-mobilization training to develop the needed skills. However, one month was a common estimate by them for the time needed. Much more training proved necessary.

The Roundout brigades spent about three months in intensive training at sites in the United States, including the National Training Center. By the time the war ended, one brigade was validated for deployment. None of the Roundout units was deployed to Southwest Asia.

By contrast, two reserve component artillery brigades did deploy to Southwest Asia. These combat support units were mobilized for about two months (including one month training at Fort Sill) before deploying. Both brigades engaged in combat, but only one, the 142nd Field Artillery Brigade, fought as a brigade.

The 142nd Brigade was notable for an aggressive peacetime leadership that achieved a very high level and intensity of peacetime training, including participation in an unusually large number of exercises with active-duty units in peacetime. The unit sustained a high level of personnel, generally in excess of 100 percent of deployment levels and managed access to and training on equipment that enabled it to operate compatibly with active artillery units.

Overall Impact of Army Guard and Reserve

In summary, the reserve components played a key role in supporting the Army's combat forces during Operations Desert Shield/Desert Storm.

Deficiencies in the pre-war readiness of the Army's combat service support and combat support units made the mobilization process longer and more difficult than expected. Despite these difficulties, these support units were made ready and performed with skill and effectiveness.

MARINE CORPS

The Marine Corps has structured its 40,000 selected reservists as a separate division consisting of the 4th Marine Division (with 50 percent of the reservists), the 4th Marine Aircraft Wing (with 25 percent) and the 4th Force Service Support Group (with 25 percent). In wartime, these units would augment or reinforce the three active-duty divisions, or provide a fourth division.

The Mobilization

The Marine Corps activated and deployed to Southwest Asia a larger percent of its available selected reserves than any other service.

- The Marine Corps activated about 30,000 selected reservists (about 75 percent of the available force). This included almost all of the combat units in the Marine 4th Division (infantry and armored units) as well as field artillery, antiaircraft artillery, aviation, intelligence and reconnaissance, combat engineering, and support units.
- About 15,000 selected reservists were in Southwest Asia at the peak of the war, representing about 17 percent of the Marine Corps in-theater strength. These units included an infantry regimental headquarters, four infantry battalions, one-plus tank battalions, six artillery batteries, and five aircraft squadrons.
- Several thousand reservists were deployed to replace active-

duty combat and support units that had deployed to Southwest Asia from the Pacific and to participate in a major training exercise in the Atlantic.

- After Operation Desert Storm began, the Marines activated almost 7,000 Individual Ready Reservists (almost 20 percent of the force) to provide replacements for anticipated casualties. None were deployed to Southwest Asia.

How the Marine Mobilization Evolved

In August 1990, the Marine view reflected their pre-war mobilization planning. It envisioned active forces able to sustain themselves for the first 60 days of a crisis. Because the reserves had no early role (and possibly no role at all), no reserve units were called up.

In October 1990, when the first reserve units were being called up, the reserves were used to provide replacements for active support units sent to Southwest Asia from other theaters and to supplement the rotation base.

By December 1990, the view of the reserves' role changed to follow the President's decision in early November to prepare for an offensive. With the increase in call-up authority to 15,000 Marine reservists on November 14, 1990, and then to 23,000 reservists on December 1, 1990, the reserves were used for two roles:

- To increase Marine amphibious and land combat capability against Iraqi forces.
- To maintain the Marines' global responsibilities in the other theaters. With no active units available in the United States to do it, this meant using reservists beyond those needed for Southwest Asia:
  - 2,300 reservists to deploy to the III Marine Expeditionary Force (MEF) in Okinawa to replace units deployed to Southwest Asia.

- 1,700 reservists to deploy to the II MEF to support a long planned NATO exercise off Norway (Battle Griffin-91).

Caught in Midst of Revitalization

When the Gulf crisis began, the Marine Corps Reserves were in the midst of a revitalization. Major improvements had been made, but the reserves had not overcome some long-standing deficiencies.

- One officer, an active-duty adviser to a tank unit, said this tank company had gone from "a bean-counting, statistics-driven, good-old-boy unit that never fired its tank guns for one 14-month period, and never even thought about mobilizing and going to war" to a unit of dedicated people focused on deployment readiness and hard training. Despite the progress, the unit still had mid-1970s tanks and had never been evaluated in the basic live fire tests of tank crew and platoon proficiency.
- Active and reserve commanders alike said that the deficiencies in the command and control of battalion-sized reserve units were linked to limited peacetime training time and the dispersed locations of subordinate units.

Making Units Ready for Deployment

The Marine Corps required that all deploying units be at a C-2 level of readiness, and said that all mobilizing units met that standard.

Unlike the Army, the Marine Corps had faith in the accuracy of the readiness reporting system because of the smallness of the force, the close supervision exercised by the active-duty Marines over the reserves, the widespread active-duty experience among

Marine Corps reserve officers, and the operation of all active-duty instructor and inspector detachments down to reserve company level.

For these reasons, coupled with the reinvigorated training program, the active Marines generally believed that small combat units such as companies, batteries and platoons were trained to do their basic wartime tasks. There was no formal validation process.

In a few cases, the Marine Corps took extraordinary measures to overcome known deficiencies in its reserve combat forces, like re-equipping two reserve tank companies and having the Army train them in the use of the M-1 tank prior to deployment.

However, at least 5 of the 20 company-sized units noted as having some training weaknesses were eventually employed in combat and continued to exist at the company and battery level— particularly in the case of the non-infantry arms such as armor and artillery.

The reserve combat units deploying to Southwest Asia underwent a 30-day pre-deployment training period at Camp Lejeune under the guidance of the 2nd Marine Division. As the Army found during its mobilization station processing of combat support and service support units, the press of time and other constraints limited what the Marine Corps could do to correct training shortcomings, or to overcome the systemic reserve component weakness in battalion-level command and control, even though unit commanders could tailor training to unit deficiencies.

Critical training limitations included:

- A lack of training equipment to replace that previously shipped to Southwest Asia.
- Too little time to train individuals in their military occupational specialties.
- Little tank gunnery or artillery live fire.
- Little company or battalion maneuver training.

In general, the Marine Corps found, as did the Army, that the mobilization station was not an efficient place to train units to acquire basic combat skills.

In-Theater Training

Once in theater, all reserve combat units were fully integrated into active units and continued to train, with an emphasis on preparing for specific missions, for example, breaching operations.

The training that enabled units to overcome pre-deployment weaknesses remained constrained by several factors:

- Reserve tank companies that were weak in gunnery skills found it difficult to improve because their live fire was limited to fixed-position, short-range firing at static targets and training ammunition was limited.
- Artillery ammunition was constrained.
- Due to their late arrival in Southwest Asia, the five reserve combat battalions were given limited time to practice battalion-level maneuver training.
- Equipment related problems, out of the control of reserve combat units, cut into the time they could spend training and so hindered their preparation for Operation Desert Storm.
  - Some pre-positioned equipment was inoperable (e.g., oil and transmission fluid seals rotted so turrets and main guns were inoperable, batteries died and tires rotted so vehicles were inoperable).
  - Some equipment shipped from the United States arrived later than the reserve units.
  - The maintenance support and spare parts needed to repair and sustain equipment were in short supply.
  - New support equipment on which units had to become proficient was issued in theater, such as the Global

Positioning System that uses satellites to pinpoint the location of units with a portable ground receiver.

Some Marine Corps units were able to correct their peacetime training deficiencies, and some were not, prior to combat:

- Active Marines still considered reserve units to be comparatively weak at effectively coordinating battalion-level operations.
- At least two of eight reserve artillery batteries improved so much that an active Marine artillery regimental commander judged them to be the best two units in his mixed active-reserve organization.
- One officer's after-action report on tank company combat said the company considered itself lucky that its training deficiencies did not lead it to serious battlefield harm.

Into Combat as Smaller Units

During Operation Desert Storm, the Marine Corps' 4th Division did not fight at division or regimental/brigade level. Five combat battalions deployed, but most were used for rear area security, for handling POWs and for regimental reserve. Only one fought in combat as a battalion.

The Marines detached companies from other battalions to engage in active combat. Twenty company-sized units (including four tank companies and six artillery batteries) fought in combat with effectiveness, initiative and courage.

Combat Support and Service Support: A Special Case

The manner in which the Marine Corps employed its reserve combat support and service support structure was directly related to the scope of Operation Desert Storm requirements and forced the Marine Corps logistics units to operate well beyond peacetime doctrine, manning and equipment levels. For example:

- Pre-Operation Desert Shield, Marine Corps truck units expected one-way line hauls of 30 to 50 miles. In Southwest Asia, truck units confronted one-way line-haul requirements of 175 to 200 miles.
- Although Operation Desert Storm required that truck units operate 24 hours per day, peacetime manning, which had reduced the number of drivers per truck in active units from 2 to 1.5, meant that the active motor transport battalions had just 60 to 70 percent of their authorized drivers. This precluded around-the-clock operations in Southwest Asia.

The extent of the inadequacy of the Marine Corps support structure became evident by early November. Then, the Marine Corps adopted a number of expedients that resulted in the call-up of about 36 percent of the Marine reserve support structure. This caused the reserve units to be employed in ways that the Marine Corps Selected Reserve commander termed less than optimal. The Marine Corps:

- Relied on the Army to haul its fuel.
- Disregarded its mobilization principle of unit replacement and integrity when it activated its only reserve motor transport battalion and then broke it up to provide drivers for the two active transport battalions, and to create a graves registration unit.
- Activated and retrained other reserve units to get 600 drivers needed to enable the remnant of the reserve motor transport battalion to meet new missions (driving commercial tractor trailers, or supervising third-country national contract drivers).
- Placed the reconstituted reserve motor transport battalion under the direction of an active-duty officer.

- Broke up its only reserve engineer battalion in order to retrain 150 of its people to be bulk fuel handlers, and attached the rest of the engineers to active units where combat engineers were in short supply.

In short, like the Army, the Marine Corps found its support structure severely stressed by the Operation Desert Storm requirements. Unlike the Army, which found it had sufficient depth in the reserve structure to meet most requirements, the Marine Corps had no depth from the beginning either in the active or reserve support structures.

Overall Impact of Marine Reserve

In summary, the Marine Corps mobilized about two-thirds of its selected reserve, including most of the 4th Division's combat units, and integrated them fully into the active-duty units. Limitations in training (and in some cases equipment) prevented the adequate preparation of battalion and regimental-sized units. Company-sized reserve combat units provided effective combat capabilities during Operation Desert Storm.

Whatever the problems and deficiencies they faced during Operation Desert Shield, Marine reserve units overcame them and performed in Operation Desert Storm with distinction.

AIR FORCE

The Air Force has structured its 200,000 guard and reserve people primarily into small units (e.g., squadrons). In wartime these units would surge their routine peacetime support to the Military Air Command (MAC) for airlift missions, to the Strategic Air Command (SAC) for air refueling missions, and to the Tactical Air Command (TAC) for tactical combat missions.

The Mobilization

The Air Force relied more heavily and earlier on its reserves than the other services:

- The Air Force activated almost 50,000 guard and reservists, about 25 percent of the available force. More than half was to support MAC by providing airlift, the rest to support TAC by providing fighter squadrons and SAC by providing air refueling. (The Air Force activated less than 1,000 members of the Individual Ready Reserve.) These guard and reserve personnel also provided communications, intelligence, aeromedical evacuation and other support.
- Approximately 11,000 guard and reserve personnel (about half guard, half reserve) were in Southwest Asia at the peak of the war. They made up an estimated 20 percent of the Air Force in-theater strength. The three reserve component combat squadrons (F-16s, A-16s, A-10s) that fought in the war made up about 5 percent of the Air Force in-theater strength.
- Many guard and reserve personnel remained in the United States to backfill units that had deployed overseas.

At the beginning of the crisis, the Air Force relied heavily on volunteers. In August 1990, volunteers from the Air Force reserve components flew 42 percent of all strategic airlift missions and 33 percent of the aerial refueling missions.

Immediately after receiving authority to call up 14,500 guard and reservists on August 23, 1990, the Air Force called to active duty three guard and three reserve squadrons to support MAC: five squadrons provided C-5s and C-141Bs for military airlift; one squadron provided airlift terminal and cargo managers. The Air Force eventually called all its reserve C-5 crews and nearly all of its C-141 crews.

In subsequent call-ups, as its authority increased to 20,000 people on November 14, 1990, the Air Force continued to emphasize non-combat units until December 1990, when it mobilized three fighter squadrons in support of TAC.

In selecting a unit to deploy, the commands relied on pre-war indicators of unit readiness (as they had been planning to do) and did not formally validate the readiness of the unit.

Tailored to Meet Requirements

The Air Force tailored its use of the guard and reserve to meet the military requirements in Southwest Asia.

- A great deal of airlift and refueling was needed to move cargo and airplanes. The active force did not have the units to do the work.
- A few combat squadrons were needed when no more active squadrons were available. Had even more combat squadrons been needed, the majority would likely have come from the Air Force Guard and Reserve.

Reserve After Active

TAC called up units from the reserve components only after it had deployed all the available active squadrons. The Air Force had decided early in the crisis to take no active units from the Pacific, no more than half of the active units from Europe, and only two squadrons from each active wing in the United States.

In December 1990, there were no more active combat units available to be deployed, so the Air Force mobilized three reserve component squadrons: F-16s from McEntire ANGB, SC; F-16s from Syracuse, NY; and A-10s from New Orleans, LA. These squadrons were picked because their engines and avionics were compatible with aircraft at the airfields in Southwest Asia that had space for them, for the quality they demonstrated in peacetime competitions, for their close ties to an active unit, and (in one case) for their unique equipment. All three squadrons were fully integrated into Operation Desert Storm.

Overall Impact of Air Force Guard and Reserve

In summary, the Air Force integrated into its active forces a critical part of its guard and reserve: many airlift and refueling squadrons, making an absolutely essential contribution to moving cargo and aircraft; a few squadrons providing combat forces beyond what the active forces could provide; and some units providing selected skills to support the deployed forces. The Air Force guard and reserve played a key role in the war outcome.

NAVY

The Navy structured its 150,000 selected reservists primarily to man any Naval Reserve Force Ships that were mobilized in a war, to provide a surge capability to support the high level of wartime operations of deployed forces, and to provide key wartime support (including medical services to handle a high level of casualties).

The Mobilization

The Navy activated and deployed to Southwest Asia fewer reservists than any other service:

- The Navy activated about 20,000 selected reservists, about 15 percent of the available force and less than 20 Individual Ready Reservists. Reservists were called primarily for their individual skills, with medical reservists comprising half of the total called.

- About 7,000 reservists were in Southwest Asia at the peak of the war, representing about 8 percent of the Navy in-theater strength. Few reservists had a combat role.

In the early weeks of August 1990, before call-up authority was given, the Navy put on active duty a small number of volunteers from the reserve. These reservists augmented logistics and cargo handling.

Immediately after getting authority on August 23, 1990, for 6,300 reservists, the Navy called up selected elements of 127 units from 34 states and the District of Columbia. Most had the mission of providing essential medical services, while others were to provide port and harbor security, sea lift support, minesweeping and shipping coordination. In subsequent call-ups, as the Navy authority increased to 30,000 reservists by December 1, 1990, its priority for reserve unit missions remained essentially the same, with medical units remaining first in priority.

In its reserve call-ups the Navy continued to emphasize selected individuals for their skills, rather than units for their roles. Unlike the other services, the Navy did not create sub-units to get access to individuals or small groups. The Navy viewed the call-up authority as permitting it to call up skilled individuals as needed, and not just entire units.

In selecting reserve units to deploy, the Navy relied on pre-war readiness indicators (as it had been planning to do) and did not formally validate the readiness of the units or individuals.

Tailored to Meet Needs

The Navy tailored its use of the reserves to meet the warfighting needs in Southwest Asia.

- Many medical people were needed. The Navy provided over

half of all medical beds in support of the Central Command, including two hospital ships and three fleet hospitals. The CENTCOM surgeon's office singled the Navy out for special praise for their responsiveness to the need for medical units.

- Few augmentees were needed for combat ships. As then envisioned, in a general war with the Soviet Union, reservists would have been used to augment active crews to support around-the-clock operations on combat ships. In the Gulf war the pace of operations was less intense. For example, aircraft carriers normally conducted flight operations about 12 hours per day.
- More minesweeping was needed. The active forces had only two of the ships needed, so the Navy activated two Naval reserve mine sweeping vessels, the *USS Adroit* and the *USS Impervious*. Once in the Gulf, they did the critical coordinated training needed with helicopters that tow mine sweeping sleds and explosive ordnance demolition teams. (The Navy did not deploy reserve air mine sweeping units, but relied on active units, which had the more modern equipment.)

Overall Impact of Navy Reserve

In summary, the Navy effectively integrated a critical part of its selected reserve with its active force: half of its medical reservists, making a major contribution to the medical service; a few units providing a capability not available in the active force; and some reservists providing selected skills to augment and support active units.

3

NAVAL QUARANTINE IN THE PERSIAN GULF CRISIS

INTRODUCTION

The initial U.S. military presence in the region consisted of the seven ships of the Joint Task Force Middle East that are permanently stationed in the Persian Gulf. On August 7, 1990, five days after the invasion, the Independence carrier battle group arrived in the Gulf of Oman and the Eisenhower carrier battle group passed through the Suez Canal en route to the Red Sea.

On August 15, ships from Maritime Prepositioned Squadron Two, based at Diego Garcia, arrived in Saudi Arabia and began to unload their cargo of military equipment and sustaining supplies for the Seventh Marine Expeditionary Brigade (MEB). Shortly thereafter military equipment and sustaining supplies for the First MEB began to arrive.

In September 1990, naval forces had increased to 52 ships, including two carrier battle groups. In addition, one battleship and the Kennedy carrier battle group were operating in the Eastern Mediterranean. In October, forces increased to 58 ships, including three carrier battle groups and four mine countermeasures ships.

In November 1990, planning and operations shifted to an offensive posture and additional ship deployments were ordered. By the time the air campaign started on January 17, the United States had 127 ships deployed in the region, including six U.S. carrier battle groups. At the time, allied navies had an additional 72 ships in the region.

THE NAVAL QUARANTINE

On August 16, U.S. Navy ships began maritime interdiction operations, the enforcement mechanism for the naval quarantine of Iraq. The first ship diversion, a Chinese vessel en route from Iraq to Qing Dao, China, occurred on August 18. As part of the coalition effort to conduct interdiction operations, 13 countries deployed naval forces to the Gulf and six additional countries provided some form of assistance.

The naval quarantine was carried out, during the war, consistent with United Nations Security Council Resolution 661 and subsequent resolutions that sought, before the war, to bring economic pressure on Iraq to withdraw from Kuwait and later to cut off the flow of war materiel.

Interdiction forces generally operated in the Persian Gulf and the Red Sea. Interdiction also involved deploying U.S. Navy units operating in the Mediterranean to identify any attempts by Algeria and Libya to provide support for Iraq or to interfere with allied operations.

Iraq is particularly susceptible to quarantine. It is a largely landlocked country with only limited access to the Persian Gulf. Before the war, approximately 60 percent of Iraqi imports arrived by sea, with the remainder arriving overland through Turkey. About 90 percent of the ocean-transported imports arrived through the Jordanian port of Aqaba on the Red Sea, and the remainder through Kuwaiti or Iraqi ports on the Persian Gulf.

Because of the Iraqi invasion of Kuwait and the presence of allied naval units in the Persian Gulf, the number of merchant ships operating in the Gulf quickly declined. Relatively few ships attempted to take cargos directly to Iraq. However, commercial traffic in the Red Sea remained high throughout Operations Desert Shield/Desert Storm. Many ships carrying embargoed cargo to the Jordanian port of Aqaba for land shipment to Iraq were intercepted and turned away.

TYPICAL INTERDICTION OPERATIONS

The Maritime Interdiction Force (MIF) continues to monitor all ocean traffic and to challenge all vessels potentially carrying contraband cargo bound for Iraq. At any given time, 10 to 15 U.S. and allied ships are directly involved in interdiction operations.

The U.S. Navy generally used the ship motor whaleboat for boardings. But in rough seas, it proved difficult to launch and to approach larger vessels. Navy crews engaged in interdiction operations expressed an urgent need for new rigid-hull, inflatable boats for boarding operations.

IMPORTANCE OF TRAINING

U.S. Navy personnel generally learned to conduct interdiction operations once they arrived in theater. Although there were some similarities with drug interdiction operations in the Caribbean, maritime interdiction operations in the Persian Gulf and the Red Sea were significantly different. Specialized training was necessary for the ships and their crews to be effective, but this requirement did not pose any difficulty.

The level of training and experience operating out of home waters were significant factors affecting individual units' effectiveness in MIF operations. For example, a U.S. commander reported that Greek and Spanish naval units had not operated out of their home waters since the 1940s which, in turn, affected their confidence when deployed to the Persian Gulf region. In a similar vein, some allied navies expressed a preference for using U.S. Navy helicopters to support MIF operations rather than their own helicopters. This preference was due primarily to a lack of experience with at-sea airborne operations.

COMMAND AND CONTROL OF MIF OPERATIONS

There was no unified command structure for ships of the thirteen allied nations that participated in naval operations during

Operations Desert Shield/Desert Storm. But the lack of a unified command structure did not prevent effective coordination and conduct of operations. Naval commanders credit a long history of joint exercises between U.S. and allied navies for the successful level of coordination achieved.

MIF STOPPED FLOW OF PROHIBITED ITEMS

To date, maritime interdiction has effectively controlled all except the smallest coastal craft movement into and out of Iraq and other ports serving as transshipping points to Iraq. Iraqi merchant ships have stopped operating in the Gulf.

The operation has virtually ended all sea commerce of prohibited items into and out of Iraq. Interdiction forces found and diverted all types of contraband cargo including missiles, precursor chemicals, command and control vehicles and assorted Soviet military equipment. The interdiction effort has also prevented other goods with military applications such as fuel additives, tires, desalination chemicals and filters and electronic components from entering Iraq. These are products the Iraqi economy is unable to produce for itself. The blockade also reduced supplies of food, clothing and refined petroleum products.

At the same time, the allied naval control of the Persian Gulf has allowed routine sea commerce to and from other nations in the Persian Gulf region to continue without interruption.

MIF EFFECT ON IRAQI WARFIGHTING UNCERTAIN

The effect of MIF operations on the ability and willingness of Iraqi forces to fight is unclear because the military services have conducted little analysis. Because such an undertaking would be difficult and perhaps ultimately inconclusive, it apparently has not even been attempted.

We do know that allied forces entering Kuwait after the war found that vehicles remaining in the country had been stripped of tires and that Iraqi soldiers were also desperately short of food and water.

These indicators can be explained in at least two ways. One is that Iraqi doctrine and operating practices may dictate against large-scale resupply efforts, or that supplies were withheld from forces in the field. The second explanation is a limited ability to resupply due to the embargo.

Given what we know of the deleterious effects of the quarantine on other sectors of the Iraqi economy, it seems reasonable to assume that the U.N.-sponsored embargo hampered Saddam's military apparatus appreciably.

4

PLANNING FOR OPERATIONS DESERT SHIELD/ DESERT STORM

INTRODUCTION

Military planning during the Cold War was focused on the prospect of a confrontation between the Soviet-led Eastern Bloc and the West, chiefly on the central front in Europe. With the end of the Cold War, this predominant planning focus is shifting and, in its wake, a more complex planning challenge is evolving. As the first major military crisis of the post–Cold War era, the war with Iraq provides a useful opportunity to analyze the planning process.

CENTCOM'S NEW PLANNING FOCUS

From its inception in 1983, the Central Command's (CENT-COM) focus had been on a Soviet invasion of Iran. Due to the Soviet withdrawal from Afghanistan and a growing appreciation of Iraq as a regional threat, CENTCOM's planning focus changed in the late 1980s. In late 1989, CENTCOM Commander in Chief General H. Norman Schwarzkopf directed CENTCOM to shift the focus of strategic planning for the region to a possible attack by Iraq on Kuwait and Saudi Arabia.

The draft contingency plan in place when Iraq invaded Kuwait in the summer of 1990 contained three phases: deterrence of an Iraqi attack against Saudi Arabia, defense of Saudi Arabia should deterrence fail, and a notional counteroffensive against Iraqi forces. Air and ground operations were integral parts of all phases of the draft plan.

Prior to the August 2, 1990 Iraqi invasion, only the first two phases of the contingency plan had been developed in any detail. The third phase detailing a counteroffensive remained undeveloped because of the CENTCOM staff's uncertainty as to how the contingency might develop and their inability to define the threat more fully. However, the notional concept for the third phase envisioned added heavy land forces to the lighter defensive forces already in place.

During the summer of 1990, a crisis simulation or exercise was conducted to test the plan in detail. This exercise involved commanders and staffs from a wide variety of units that would be assigned to CENTCOM in the event of an actual war. The specific plan tested in this exercise focused on a threatened attack by Iraq through Kuwait into Saudi Arabia. That plan provided for deployment of the equivalent of 4 2/3 Army and Marine divisions focused around the Army's XVIII Airborne Corps and a Marine Expeditionary Force. It would be supported by 15 U.S. Air Force tactical fighter squadrons and three U.S. Navy carrier battle groups.

Based on this exercise, planners recognized that the U.S. force would require additional heavy armored forces in order to counter large Iraqi mechanized forces. Consequently, planners added another heavy division to the contingency plan's order of battle.

CENTCOM's ability to plan for and ultimately execute with confidence Operation Desert Storm was enhanced by years of U.S. presence in the Persian Gulf region. Significant security assistance programs, land and sea-based prepositioned supplies, and a significant naval presence since the 1987 tanker escorting operations during the Iran-Iraq war are just some examples of the many planning and operational advantages CENTCOM enjoyed.

PLANNING THE AIR CAMPAIGN

The draft CENTCOM plan included deployment of air forces into the theater as a deterrent force and, if necessary, to conduct counter-air and air-interdiction operations against Iraqi forces. The planning concept for the U.S. counteroffensive included a strategic air campaign.

However, the CENTCOM plan did not provide for a specific and detailed air campaign against Iraq. The Operation Desert Storm offensive air campaign plan—characterized by devastating, simultaneous attacks on political, military and industrial targets in Iraq and on Iraqi forces in Kuwait—did not exist as anything more than a concept prior to August 2, 1990.

There have been valid criticisms of the pre-war plan's detailed focus on defense and deterrence instead of offensive operations. Although General Schwarzkopf had correctly identified the threat to the region, he decided that the third phase of the plan should remain vague. In hindsight, it would have been better to have planned the strategic air campaign in advance, because the majority of the targets were fixed and could have been identified. Even though aircraft were in theater within days after the invasion, the lack of a detailed offensive plan would have hampered effective air operations had they been required at that time.

Detailed planning within CENTCOM Headquarters for an air campaign began immediately after August 2, and emphasized a defensive air campaign in the event that Iraq invaded Saudi Arabia. However, it did not take long for air planning to shift to the offense. Within the first week following the decision to deploy U.S. forces to Saudi Arabia, a planning cell within the Air Staff in Washington developed a more detailed approach for a strategic air campaign.

The Air Staff's approach focused on attacking critical Iraqi "centers of gravity" that, it was hoped, might lead to the withdrawal of Iraqi forces from Kuwait and the destruction of Iraq's nuclear, biological and chemical capabilities. Following a briefing of the conceptual plan with General Schwarzkopf, the concept was further developed, and the Air Staff planning cell was augmented by staff officers from the other services. The plan prepared by the Air Staff was then taken to the theater, where it was used by the

Central Command Air Force (CENTAF) planning staff as a baseline to develop CENTCOM's more detailed and more focused offensive air campaign plan.

The plan envisioned a phased application of air power, first to obtain air superiority, then to attack Iraq's command and control and warmaking potential, and finally, to prepare the battlefield in the Kuwaiti theater of operations (KTO). Initially focused on some 84 targets in Iraq and the Kuwaiti theater of operations, the plan had grown to 174 targets by September 13 when General Schwarzkopf decided that the offensive air campaign plan was ready.

Throughout the period of Operation Desert Shield, a continuous dialogue took place among the CENTAF planners, the Air Staff's "Checkmate" planning cell and the Navy's "Spear" intelligence group as the process of identifying strategic targets continued and the plan evolved. Important details of the final plan were not decided for several months. By the time the air campaign began on January 17, 1991, the plan had grown to include 386 separate targets and would ultimately grow to 723 targets.

One issue that arose during the planning of the air campaign was whether or not the use of air power alone could achieve U.S. military and political objectives in the Gulf. Instant Thunder (as this air-only plan was called) was not executed, however, because senior military planners and DOD officials believed that an air-only option could not guarantee the withdrawal of the Iraqi army from Kuwait.

PLANNED AIR CAMPAIGN HAD FOUR PHASES

CENTCOM's air campaign plan for Operation Desert Storm was composed of four phases. The first, or strategic phase, was intended to: destroy Iraq's integrated air defense system, gain air superiority over the Iraqi air force, destroy Iraq's strategic offensive capabilities (nuclear, biological and chemical weapons and production facilities and SCUD tactical ballistic missiles, launchers, and production capabilities), and disrupt Iraqi command, control and communications to its armed forces.

Phase II was intended to suppress Iraqi air defenses in the KTO to provide freedom of action for Phase III attacks against Iraqi Regular Army and Republican Guards in the KTO. The Phase III attacks were meant to isolate the Iraqi army in the KTO, cut it off from its source of resupply and reinforcements, and then reduce it to the level that a ground campaign could be conducted with minimal casualties. Phase IV provided air support to the ground offensive.

PLANNING FOR THE GROUND OFFENSIVE

Planning for the ground offensive campaign began almost immediately after the Iraqi invasion and was done on a close-hold, compartmented basis by small planning cells in both CENTCOM and the Pentagon. For about three months, knowledge of the planning was limited to a handful of senior officials.

In early October, the CENTCOM ground plan called for penetration of Iraqi defenses in Kuwait and a relatively shallow envelopment to the west to trap Iraqi forces. Although the exact numbers of Iraqi troops were unknown, their strength steadily increased throughout the fall and their defenses extended farther and farther west.

CENTCOM recognized that conducting a shallow envelopment with the number of allied forces in theater and against the ever-stronger Iraqi forces had problems. The available U.S. and allied ground forces restricted the scope of a ground attack to a fairly direct drive into Iraqi defenses. However, CENTCOM believed it was the only executable ground campaign with the forces on hand. A wider envelopment would have caused the attacking force to be split, leaving both elements dangerously exposed to attack by Iraqi reserves. The shortcomings of this plan fostered recognition of the need for additional ground forces.

On November 8, 1990, the President announced his decision to increase U.S. forces in theater to provide a more effective offensive option. With the decision to deploy the VII Corps from Europe, CENTCOM planners developed a more detailed ground offensive plan that began to take the form of the campaign that was ultimately conducted. Additional forces meant that the envelopment could be shifted farther to the west to circumvent the strength of the Iraqi defenses, envelop the Iraqi Army in Kuwait and destroy the Republican Guard operational reserve in southeastern Iraq.

This maneuver became known as the "Left Hook." It was to be conducted in concert with the threat of an amphibious assault on the Kuwaiti coast to focus Iraqi attention to the east and supporting attacks by Marines and pan-Arab forces in the center to hold Iraqi tactical reserves in place.

The assumption of a successful air campaign was integral to planning for the ground campaign. The air campaign was to reduce Iraqi ground units by at least 50 percent and Iraqi artillery by 90 percent in those areas where breaching operations were anticipated.

Perhaps because of the compartmented nature of the planning process, there are conflicting reports about the origins of the "Left Hook," which was intended to capitalize on the superior ability of U.S. forces to concentrate allied combat power against Iraqi vulnerabilities.

LOW CASUALTIES THE HIGHEST GOAL

In planning Operation Desert Storm, minimizing allied and civilian casualties was the highest priority. From the outset of the planning effort, air power was intended to be fully employed to prepare the battlefield. Likewise, planning for the ground campaign was to avoid Iraqi strengths and rely instead on deception and maneuver to apply our strengths against Iraqi vulnerabilities. Deploying overwhelming U.S. military force in the theater and doing nothing to provoke a ground war before U.S. and allied forces were ready also proved invaluable to CENTCOM's objective of minimizing casualties in the conflict.

As mentioned, deception was a key element of Operation Desert Storm and, in particular, of the ground campaign. The objective of the deception was to convince the Iraqi leadership and army that the coalition forces would attack directly into the Iraqi defenses in Kuwait, engaging in the battles of attrition that characterized the Iran-Iraq War. This, in turn, would result in high U.S. casualties.

When the VII Corps deployed into the theater from Europe, it occupied tactical assembly areas in the southeast. The VII Corps and the already-deployed XVIII Corps delayed their movement to the west until early February 1991, at which time the covert move commenced. CENTCOM's plan called for a feint by the 1st Cavalry Division to reinforce the deception of the major coalition ground attack being initiated in this central sector. Likewise, a small Marine Task Force would mask a move westward by the 1st and 2nd Marine Divisions. Marines afloat in the Persian Gulf would provide the credible threat of an amphibious landing on the coast and tie down several Iraqi divisions in the east.